God's Poems

God's Poems

The Beauty of Poetry
and the Christian Imagination

JOHN POCH

ST. AUGUSTINE'S PRESS
South Bend, Indiana

Manufactured in the United States of America.

1 2 3 4 5 6   27 26 25 24 23 22

Library of Congress Control Number: 2021950331

Paperback ISBN: 978-1-58731-342-4
Ebook ISBN: 978-1-58731-346-2

∞ The paper used in this publication meets the minimum
requirements of the American National Standard for Information Sciences –
Permanence of Paper for Printed Materials, ANSI Z39.48-1984.

St. Augustine's Press
www.staugustine.net

That later we, though parted then,
May still recall these evenings when
Fear gave his watch no look;
The lion griefs loped from the shade
And on our knees their muzzles laid,
And Death put down his book.
—W.H. Auden

Contents

To the Glory of God

Introduction

How does one read a poem? Anyone can begin to read a poem if that person knows how to read sentences. And yet, it's not quite *that* easy. One must also begin to recognize more complicated aspects of language such as metaphor, various types of rhyme, allusion, irony, chiasmus, meter, etc. Just as with playing piano or riding a bike, anyone can get better at an activity with some knowledge and instruction concerning the intricate details of how the instrument or vehicle works. And with the guidance of friends, parents, teachers, coaches, and pastors, one can become more expert, efficient, and even adventurous at deeper intellectual exercise. And with practice, one becomes familiar with the various possibilities.

As with the piano or the bicycle, you should enjoy the experience. If you don't feel something, you're missing the entire point. Sure, the bicycle can get you somewhere, practically speaking, but most people riding bikes aren't doing it only practically but for fun. Though many a child facing another practice might take issue, the piano was meant for pure pleasure, though it can also transport us. This book means to offer an insight into that kind of enjoyment: how the language and form of good poems work, and also to give some perspective into how I see some of my favorite poems developing beyond simple beauty toward spiritual truths. This is simply (and complicatedly) a book about how to read poems.

If you are reading these introductory paragraphs, you are a reader of prose. You know how sentences work in English, how one word leads into another and the functions of the parts of speech. You might even have a sense of the rhythms and repetitions and sounds of a sentence. Even poets have a hard time defining the difference between prose and poetry, because so often prose can be quite poetic. And we have a genre called the "prose poem" which is more poem than story, somehow more or other than narrative. It is, however, usually an insult if a poem is called prosaic. So, there is a difference. But the line between prose and poetry is not always clearly defined.

Another word for poetry is "verse." Reading verse is not the same thing as reading prose. *Verse* comes from a Latin word meaning simply *to turn,* as in the way a farmer with a plow would turn at the end of a row. Poets turn back along a line of poetry and intentionally plow another line in the same way, conscious of making a line in parallel with the prior one. Metaphorically, we might think of this plowing as preparation for a fruitful harvest of meaning.

The word *prose* oddly enough comes from the term *pro versa* signifying: to go away from turning. A line of prose wraps near the edge of the page; there is no intentional turn by the writer of prose. It is defined by the size of the page and the placement of the margin. The printer, not the writer, is in charge here. For the writer of prose, the sentence and accrual of sentences move forward toward the point or the end of a collection of thoughts, but not toward a specifically intended turn of a line. This travel is more like a distant journey rather than the farming of one's own plot. Perhaps a poem hits closer to home than prose?

A poem is more akin to travel that turns in a more confined space: plowing, dancing, or even a football game could be metaphors for this dynamic: organized back and forth movements in order to achieve some profitable or entertaining goal. It is like theater compared to a film. You are confined to the very limited space of the stage to achieve your goals. A film can traverse continents or outer space in its locales, but the stage creates a different kind of limitation for the actor and director. Verse readers appreciate the compression of this space and look for turns within it. I like to think of poems as artworks that develop noticeable patterns or repetitions—especially repetitions with variations.

Early in childhood, there is something pleasing to us in our most primitive moments of language cognition when we hear a rhyme. Is there a child who doesn't love Dr. Seuss's constant rhyming? "I do not like them / in a house. / I do not like them with a mouse. / I do not like them / here or there. / I do not like them. / Anywhere. / I do not like green eggs and ham. / I do not like them Sam-I-am." As you can see (or hear) here, a rhyme is merely a repetition of sound, usually including some kind of variation. Avoiding monotony, it is pleasing due to that variation's surprise.

Howard Nemerov's poem "Because You Asked About the Line Between Prose and Poetry" tries to get at this impossible distinction between verse and prose, as only poetry can. The poem opens:

Sparrows were feeding in a freezing drizzle
That while you watched turned to pieces of snow
Riding a gradient invisible
From silver aslant to random, white, and slow.

There is a shift of perception as the drizzle turns to snow and the silver to white. And then, the further shift:

There came a moment that you couldn't tell.
And then they clearly flew instead of fell.

Is it simply that poetry is language that defies gravity? That flies (as in the last line)? Or is it more lodged in the moment (the penultimate line) when you can't quite tell what is what? What is flying at the end: the snow or the sparrows or both? Poetry is often about the *not* knowing, about the suspension between two worlds. If you like suspense, the excitement of being in the moment, you might like poetry.

***

Many through the ages have considered poetry, of all the various expressions available to us (dancing, painting, music, fiction, photography, film, etc.), the highest form of art. Perhaps this has to do with a poet making more with less. Economy has long been one of the virtues of a well-made poem. No words are wasted. That's not to say that words are wasted in a good novel. No fiction writer worth her salt would allow padding of the pages with unnecessary language. Yet poetry has a kind of density to it that is similar to an essence or a perfume. The phrasings, imagery, and lines have staying power. When you peel an orange, you eat the interior. That's prose. But fifteen minutes later, when the taste in your mouth is long gone, when you smell the essence of the peel on your fingers, that's poetry.

People don't memorize novels and rarely do they remember sentences from those novels. But many can call to mind lines and stanzas of poetry and even entire poems: the exact language rather than the idea the words elicit. Poetry is like scripture in this way; it wants to be quoted. There is something beautiful about the words themselves—not just what happens through a combination of plot, scene, characters, or theme. Though poems can have plots, as well.

3

Christian believers who have grown up exposed to the scriptures have had practice with poems whether they know it or not. The books of *Job, Psalms, Proverbs, Isaiah, the Gospel of John, The Song of Solomon,* and *Revelation* are full of verse and poetic language. And most of the other books of the Bible partake of poetry in some measure, even if they were originally written as letters. As well, hymns and praise songs are created with the rhythms of poetic language we find most beautiful and useful for conveying the simplicity and intricacy of Godly truths.

The Greek word *poeima* means "the made thing." In Ephesians 2:10, Paul refers to each human being as God's *poeima*. Some translations call this God's "workmanship" or "handiwork." It might be more interesting to translate closer to the Greek and see that we are, each of us, God's poem. (*God's Poems*—sounds like a really nice title.) You might then think of Him as the finest Poet writing His best work, feeling and thinking deeply, marveling at the creation of each human. If we are, as Genesis 1:26 declares, made in God's image, then our very nature is a creative one. After all, the first thing God does in Genesis is create a world. So then, logically, we ought to, at heart, be creative ourselves. Often I hear people say, "Oh, I'm not a creative person." But to *not* be creative is missing the mark of our full potential. Not everyone should write poems for a living, but we were all made to make.

This awareness of the power, necessity, and art of language is at the core of who we are. In Genesis, we see the poetic nature of who we might be from the very beginning, specifically God giving the task of naming to the first man. We ought to take it seriously. And playfully. Poems are little worlds unto themselves. Each poet creates a world with only a few words. In nearly the same way, by words, God commands the universe into existence. Of course, man's creation is a metaphysical one. Only God can create matter out of nothing, though you can't say the theoretical physicists and magicians don't try to create the illusion.

When Paul famously addresses the men of Athens on Mars Hill, his apologetics are not only intellectual or experiential; they are poetic. His rhetoric connects to his audience through his knowledge of their religion, philosophy, and the arts of sculpture and poetry. Specifically, he says in Acts 17: 28, "for in Him we live and move and have our being, as also some of your own poets have said, 'For we are also His offspring.'" While Paul does note the differences between his religion and the Greek pagans, he finds common ground with them in their art. He knows that he can build a relationship with them upon the idea that all truth is God's truth, even poetic truth. In our contemporary worship services today, with the lights dimmed in the sanctuary, many pastors use clips from movies on screens above the altar to get their points across to the congregation. From the silliness of the *Princess Bride* to the harrowing power of *Silence*, the art of film connects with people. My own pastor, much to my delight, cites some kind of poem in nearly every sermon. Sometimes the poems are clearly devotional poems, but sometimes they are contemporary poems that express powerfully human feeling, suffering, joy, and pain. Yes, even the truth found in secular art can glorify God. Beyond his deliberate mention of pagan poetry at the Areopagus, Paul himself is somewhat of a poet, writing his letters with an extraordinarily poetic prose.

What good are poems? It's a fair question. Most people seem to survive without much poetry their entire lives. Nearly everybody writes a poem at some point, but truly, very few read them unless they are forced to do so in some required college class. Nevertheless, poems are essential. Especially for the Christian, who has God's very word revealed through this genre, this style, this repetition with variation whether by rhyme, metaphor, anaphora, allusion, etc. If we don't understand how poems in general work, how could we possibly understand how the poetry of scripture works? If we can't tell a good love poem from a bad one, how can we know whether the poetry of the psalmist is effective? I tell students: Weak poems such as those on Hallmark cards are useful in that they give us what we expect; great poems that we consider to be literature give us what we never expected. They go beyond the usefulness of conveying a feeling and unveiling beauty; and they tell us who we are.

At the university where I work, usually, unfortunately, my first job in a poetry classroom is to un-teach students what they believe a poem is. Most students come in with the idea that a poem is no more than an expression of raw emotion having to do with death, alienation, love, sex, and/or family. I tell them: what you are describing is *Keeping Up with the Kardashians*. The one thing usually missing from this initial conversation is that poems are a language construct. "What about words?" I ask them. So we get back to basics, and we begin again by talking about foundational aspects like parts of speech, line breaks, metaphors, and sentences. Pretty boring stuff, as elements may seem boring to a chemistry student. However, all one needs is a little covalent bonding to allow an interesting mathematics to arise. Pronouns might seem fairly dull, but a poem can use the right pronoun in the right spot to transform a world. I do like point out to these same students that a conflict on *Keeping up with the Kardashians* usually results in the failure of language, and cursing (yet another language failure) whereas in a good poem, language emerges fully formed. We witness in poetry the control of language, not the chaos. There is a good reason Paul tells the Romans to "bless and curse not." It could be the difference between building a world rather than tearing one down.

Romantic notions of poetry have some measure of truth in them, but poems should be as beautiful intellectually as they are emotionally—probably more so of the mind than the heart since language is more likely to be used as communication than expression. Poems are where the mind and heart meet, perhaps on equal terms. I have had many students in my creative writing courses over the years who claim, "I write for myself." I kindly let them know that if this is their approach, they ought to find another class because the course requires that I be a reader of their work along with the other students. So, we have an audience. The truth is, no one writes for only themselves; when we write poetry, we want to communicate (even if subconsciously) something to a friend, a lover, a rival, an audience of our peers, or the entire world. Or our better selves, our better angels. Or God.

Poetry is poorly taught in elementary schools and high schools around the country. I know this because I inherit so many of these students who, in order to get a good grade, want to know or proclaim the meaning of a poem. They want to sum it up. They have been taught that a poem has a meaning. Yet there is no singular meaning to a poem. A poem has a multiplicity of meaning operating in every line and stanza throughout a poem. We might be able to say that there is a clear theme to a poem or an emotional tenor, but no poem has a single meaning. It's a relief, then, to most of my students who are able to interpret or comment on a poem differently than their peers and still possibly be "right" in their viewpoint. A poem is not a mathematical equation which has one answer. Rather than quantitative, the poem is qualitative in its variety of answers and revelations. This is not to say that any interpretation is true. Sylvia Plath's poem "Daddy" could not be considered a praise poem to the Christian God or a poem about shoes. If you think either of these things, you are a poor reader. And yet the "father" of her poem could be seen by turns as the speaker's father, husband, the Christian God, the Devil, and/or the entire Western patriarchy, depending on how you're reading the various lines.

I don't blame teachers, per se, as it is more of a systemic problem that is exacerbated by our culture of testing, assessment regimes, and that sort of thing. Teachers often teach to the test or even to the fact that students will be taught continuously throughout their education toward other tests. They need solid answers. They are no doubt preparing their students for "real life," and they are often forced into these strictures. However, you can't test students quantitatively on their poetry knowledge and skills in the same way you can test biology or math or history, which has clear and quantitative answers. The answers to a poem (if those even exist) are often qualitative and could be multiple.

To say that a poem has a meaning is like saying to a student, "Here's a key: Now go find a lock that fits." This is obviously a backwards approach. Much better to say: this poem is a kind of treasure chest with a lock. Here are a whole set of keys or tools and techniques of picking this lock. And once that lock is open, there is a box of meaning available to you that may very well be full of treasure. You also have to have the patience to realize the box may be empty, or it may have something in it that is of no value to you whatsoever. At the same time, it may be of great value to someone else. The joy of opening that lock can be half the fun. But a poem is not simply a lock or a puzzle to be picked once and for all. Inside the treasure chest of a great poem is also another treasure map leading you on to other treasure chests. It's that complicated and that fun.

No Christian can deny the importance of words. Believers understand that God names and we name. Speaking and naming are two different things; God speaks the world into existence, but then he names, which seems to me a more personal action. My pastor recently pointed out to me that, in Hebrew, initially Adam's name is not just his name, but it also means "the Adam," implying that God creates a kind of human before identifying it as male. So Adam is first creature, then person, who is then male who then needs a female, a woman, Eve, whose name means "life-giver." We know that the name Adam, also means "earth," implying "of the ground." This multiplicity of who we are, from the beginning, in just a name, should signal us to the fact that names are not only important, but extremely complex in order to show us our wide potential.

In the second chapter of Genesis, we see Adam given the task of naming cattle, birds, and beast. And after that, he even names Woman as a kind of rhyme with himself, Man. In a poem, no less:

This is now bone of my bones
And flesh of my flesh;
She shall be called Woman,
Because she was taken out of Man.

We do not write poems in a vacuum, but we repeat language while making it new. In the very first verse of John's Gospel, John begins by imitating the first verse of the Bible by writing: "In the beginning was the Word." There can be no doubt the writer knew exactly what he was doing by repeating from Genesis 1 (with variation): "In the beginning, God…" By this variation, John is able to make a profound link to Jesus as God, beyond teacher and prophet, physician and friend, poet and storyteller, though clearly Jesus is those things, as well. John is also evangelizing his Greek audience who believed in a nameless, creative power behind all the ordering of the universe, whom they referred to as "the word" or "logos."

My hope is that by reading these poems (and my take on them as a kind of guidance along with my observations and anecdotes), you will not only enjoy the poems for the spiritual truths they reveal (yes, reveal, as in *revelation*). You will also become more adept at noticing the poetic beauty of language wherever you find it—especially in scripture. Some of the poems are secular and written by nonbelievers, yet they still contain valuable spiritual truths. Developing our attention to how words work can only help us read scripture better, to pray with clearer petitions and more beautiful phrases which God, aka the Word, surely would appreciate. The French theologian, Simone Weil, wrote a wonderful essay called "Reflections on the Right Use of School Studies" in which she argues that, even if you don't enjoy geometry or won't use geometry in your practical life, through working out the problems (even if you fail at getting the right answer) you can still learn a kind of practice of attention. A devotion to any given problem itself develops our intellect for something much greater than the material directly at hand. She argues that this kind of development of attention of the mind is key to being able to have an attentive prayer life. And what could be better than that? It is the same with poetry, only even more spiritual than geometry because words have a more direct link to the divine. Genesis doesn't tell us the world was created by geometry or chemistry.

One need not study theology at a seminary to understand how scripture works, though that doesn't hurt. By reading ordinary and extraordinary poems, one learns how exegesis works. Believers understand there is a difference in reading a secular poem and a God-inspired poem. You can go out on a limb and wildly misinterpret a poem by T.S. Eliot, and not have it affect much of anything; you're just a bad reader. If you misinterpret a scripture, it can be detrimental to your life and the lives of others. *Exegesis* is a fancy word for interpretation that has its roots in meaning "to lead" or "to guide." Much like a pastor who longs to share the good news of the gospel, as a poetry teacher I have a desire to lead and guide others to see the beauty in an excellent poem. I want to share it. In most of the chapters here, I try to look closely at poems and marvel at how they work.

***

I loved books from an early age, but it wasn't until well into college that I ever thought I might write one. And early on, I hardly read poetry. I read stories and novels. I did not always think I would become a poet, though in the third grade, in 1976, I did win an award for a silly patriotic poem I wrote for a Bicentennial competition organized by our elementary school. In fact, I didn't read poetry seriously until much later. My intellectual talents in high school were mostly mathematical, and my early inclinations were that I might be an architect, computer scientist, or some kind of engineer. I was a first-generation college student, so I really had little clue as to how college and an ensuing career might take shape. This worked in my favor, I suppose, as I was free to flounder about for a while. My first two years of college were full of chemistry, physics, and calculus, though it was an art history class at Clayton State College that drew my attention to the idea of beauty. I will never forget Professor Ludley's excitement over the color of the beautiful woman's hair in a Pre-Raphaelite painting or the attention to the extraordinary and pronounced line of the Neo-Classicists.

His deep interest in and passion for beauty infected me. I also was required to take a few English courses where I was exposed to short stories and poetry, and this study of literature built on the small amount of reading I had done in high school.

After two years of college, when my parents suddenly separated, I moved to Scottsdale, Arizona to help my mother get through a very difficult time. This required that I drop out of school for a year. Since money was scarce, when I wasn't delivering pizzas I spent most of my leisure time at the local pool or at the public library where I found it deeply satisfying to escape my fallen world by reading fiction and poetry. I began writing my own stories and sending them off to *The New Yorker* and *The Atlantic*. I had no clue what it took to be a writer. I was as naïve as they come. When I returned to Georgia, I enrolled at Georgia Tech to pursue nuclear engineering, but my heart wasn't in it. For the first time in my life, I did poorly in my studies. I had always been an A student, but now the center would not hold. Things fell apart.

Some of this had to do with my working 30–40 hours a week on the Southeastern Freight Lines loading dock, moving freight from one trailer to another. But mostly my fault was writing poems rather than studying enough for my statics class or for nuclear physics. Then I discovered that you could study poetry and fiction writing just down the road at Georgia State University where I had witnessed W.S. Merwin read his poems one evening. To this day, Merwin remains one of my favorite poets. In short order, I enrolled in David Bottoms' Saturday morning poetry workshop, and my life was changed. I had found my calling.

Again, it's not that simple. I had grown up in the church. Hearing the scriptures proclaimed every week, those cadences and rhythms, the hymns and praise songs—that was my first introduction to poetry. I remember how years ago a poetry mentor became exasperated at my stringing together prepositional phrase after prepositional phrase. "Where did I get this bad habit?" he asked. I didn't have a clue, until some time afterward I noticed the problem when I became frustrated in my reading of a long, drawn out and complicated sentence. This sentence was in some epistle of the Apostle Paul who was piling on prepositions like they might just run out if he didn't get them written down in one gorgeous string of meaning layered on meaning.

Another influence: my Poppop (my mother's father) fancied himself a poet, though he had never really published much beyond small newspapers. But he could quote poems and was a free spirit unlike most of the rest of us practical people in the family. I remember he used to roam the country and hang out in college cafeterias just to be around young people. Poppop loved traveling around the United States to see his five kids and many grandkids, and he told jokes and little stories and anecdotes that entertained just about anybody he met. But from the beginning, I knew the kind of poetry I would write and love would be more serious and difficult and even depressing. I was not in this for entertainment, as my grandfather was; this was for me a matter of life and death.

Nevertheless, I consider myself to be a witty poet, often playing with a multiplicity of meanings, even punning. At least I have been accused by a few critics of being witty, as if that were only a negative thing. This wit I probably inherited from my father's side. Every year for our summer vacation, we traveled to Delaware to visit my grandparents there. As a small child, my grandmother came to America with her family as part of the great exodus from Eastern Europe, escaping the Bolshevik Revolution. Her parents spoke Russian, and she grew up speaking it as well. As a first-generation immigrant, she had a capacity with language that even I can't fully imagine. She knew some Hungarian and various Russian dialects, if I remember correctly. She taught us Russian phrases such as "Praise the Lord" and "The rabbit is in the cabbage." I am sure much of my love of language, especially the play of it, was passed down from her. I remember my grandmother always punning. Her one-liners are legendary among our family. We went to Delaware every year for our week-long summer vacation. Every morning, as we came down the stairs and into the kitchen for our breakfasts, she would announce: "Good morning glory, have you seen the rain, dear?"

***

Purposefully, I have chosen an extremely wide range of poems for this book. Some begin with the premise that we live in a world created by a living and loving God. Some are secular and do not acknowledge God as an intimate being, or pretend for a minute that He is or was ever here or anywhere to begin with. Yet all these poems seem to me to yearn for Him and His love and His life, even in their denials. Some are longer poems of free verse, but many work in traditional formal modes. I try to describe briefly how some of these poems use form and function, but for a more detailed introductory book on poetic form and meter, if you are interested, I suggest a book by Alfred Corn called *The Poem's Heartbeat*. There are, of course, many others to choose from.

I am particularly fond of more traditionally "formal" poems, in part because, as a poet, I tend to work often within those strictures. But more importantly, I find these poems particularly interesting in that they often show to the reader, through their architectural forms and patterns, how they create and reveal meaning. I intentionally have chosen poems from antiquity to present to show that poems of spiritual beauty have a long tradition. I especially have chosen mostly contemporary poems in English to show how vital poetry is today, even though Americans, in general, do not read much poetry by living writers. This should not be so, though it is understandable. Reading poetry is hard work and takes time.

Poetry may seem like the ideal medium in a world of such short attention spans, because poems are usually just a page or two long. Compare this to a reader's commitment to a novel! Yet, this one page of poetry, due to its complex beauty can be stifling to a reader who isn't prepared. People are used to multitasking inside of multitasking. You can tweet while you watch TV (flipping between two football games at once) and iron clothes. But you can't read a poem and at the same time do much of anything else. Like God, poems require all of you: heart, mind, and body. Poems are difficult, but the payoff can be absolutely unlike any other artistic experience. The experience of holding so much knowledge and beauty in your mind and heart at once is a great accomplishment and reward for a reader.

Some of these chapters have grown out of reviews or other published essays that I have written in my vocation as a poetry critic/reviewer. In most instances I have taken my former observations or criticisms of the various poems and geared them toward a larger exegesis and vision, seeing them in a more spiritual light.

***

Throughout this book, I use the New King James translation of the Holy Bible. To my ear, the music of the English language is at one of its great heights in the Renaissance (Shakespeare, Donne, and Herbert, among others), and this is the same time period that the King James translation was initially done. The Bible that I have used for years is the Geneva (or Reformed) Study Bible. You will likely notice many of my own perspectives and insights overlap with this wonderful version directed by R.C. Sproul. Pastor Dale Smith gave me this Bible as a gift when he hardly even knew me. I suppose he could sense that I loved words, and he thought it important that I have good insight into these words. What an extraordinary example of Christian brotherhood! His gift changed my life more than any other book ever given to me. This version and its extraordinary notes and references have been a lifeline and a mentor to me through high and low, thick and thin, hell and high water.

***

Acknowledgments:

Some of these essays (or parts of them) were published in these journals:

Alabama Literary Review, America, American Literary Review, Christianity and Literature, Five Points, Sewanee Theological Review, Smartish Pace, and *The Writer's Chronicle.*

I am grateful to Texas Tech University for giving me a generous scholarship catalyst grant to work on this book, and to the Virginia Center for the Creative Arts who provided me with a generous residency where I was able to work uninterrupted.

Pastors, in my experience, (besides acting as helpful and faithful shepherds to their flocks) are the guardians and stewards of the words of faith. They care deeply about the complex, difficult, and marvelous revelations of language, and they know that often, when a sentence, a line, or even a word is spoken, it is loaded with a multiplicity of meaning. I have been helped by pastors throughout my life in understanding scripture, and perhaps now I can offer something in return, iron sharpening iron along the edge of truth and beauty. I am grateful to all of them who, through various times of my life, have given me encouragement and instructions in the Word and for the world, especially David Cooper, Matt Gordon, Tommy Nelson, Dale Smith, Jerry Saliba, Chuck Williams, Doug Halcomb, Mike Martindale, Baron Eliason, Tyson Taylor, Matt Young, and Elliott Powell.

The sacrifices that most pastors make daily for others are extraordinary, beautiful, and demanding.

Also, my thanks goes out to students, friends, and colleagues who love the Word and words and have challenged me to push further and dig deeper. Some of them read early versions of these essays and gave me solid help in revision. They are too many to name. My wife, Meghan, of course, is an abiding force of love who keeps me moving forward.

Poetry from the Beginning: Genesis 1

1 In the beginning God created the heavens and the earth. ²The earth was without form, and void; and darkness *was* on the face of the deep. And the Spirit of God was hovering over the face of the waters.

³Then God said, "Let there be light"; and there was light. ⁴And God saw the light, that *it was* good; and God divided the light from the darkness. ⁵God called the light Day, and the darkness He called Night. So the evening and the morning were the first day.

⁶Then God said, "Let there be a firmament in the midst of the waters, and let it divide the waters from the waters." ⁷Thus God made the firmament, and divided the waters which *were* under the firmament from the waters which *were* above the firmament; and it was so. ⁸And God called the firmament Heaven. So the evening and the morning were the second day.

⁹Then God said, "Let the waters under the heavens be gathered together into one place, and let the dry *land* appear"; and it was so. ¹⁰And God called the dry *land* Earth, and the gathering together of the waters He called Seas. And God saw that *it was* good.

¹¹Then God said, "Let the earth bring forth grass, the herb *that* yields seed, *and* the fruit tree *that* yields fruit according to its kind, whose seed *is* in itself, on the earth"; and it was so. ¹²And the earth brought forth grass, the herb *that* yields seed according to its kind, and the tree *that* yields fruit, whose seed *is* in itself according to its kind. And God saw that *it was* good. ¹³So the evening and the morning were the third day.

¹⁴Then God said, "Let there be lights in the firmament of the heavens to divide the day from the night; and let them be for signs and seasons, and

for days and years; ¹⁵ and let them be for lights in the firmament of the heavens to give light on the earth"; and it was so. ¹⁶ Then God made two great lights: the greater light to rule the day, and the lesser light to rule the night. *He made* the stars also. ¹⁷ God set them in the firmament of the heavens to give light on the earth, ¹⁸ and to rule over the day and over the night, and to divide the light from the darkness. And God saw that *it was* good. ¹⁹ So the evening and the morning were the fourth day.

²⁰ Then God said, "Let the waters abound with an abundance of living creatures, and let birds fly above the earth across the face of the firmament of the heavens." ²¹ So God created great sea creatures and every living thing that moves, with which the waters abounded, according to their kind, and every winged bird according to its kind. And God saw that *it was* good. ²² And God blessed them, saying, "Be fruitful and multiply, and fill the waters in the seas, and let birds multiply on the earth." ²³ So the evening and the morning were the fifth day.

²⁴ Then God said, "Let the earth bring forth the living creature according to its kind: cattle and creeping thing and beast of the earth, *each* according to its kind"; and it was so. ²⁵ And God made the beast of the earth according to its kind, cattle according to its kind, and everything that creeps on the earth according to its kind. And God saw that *it was* good.

²⁶ Then God said, "Let Us make man in Our image, according to Our likeness; let them have dominion over the fish of the sea, over the birds of the air, and over the cattle, over all[b] the earth and over every creeping thing that creeps on the earth." ²⁷ So God created man in His *own* image; in the image of God He created him; male and female He created them. ²⁸ Then God blessed them, and God said to them, "Be fruitful and multiply; fill the earth and subdue it; have dominion over the fish of the sea, over the birds of the air, and over every living thing that moves on the earth."

²⁹ And God said, "See, I have given you every herb *that* yields seed which *is* on the face of all the earth, and every tree whose fruit yields seed; to you it shall be for food. ³⁰ Also, to every beast of the earth, to every bird of the air, and to everything that creeps on the earth, in which *there is* life, *I*

have given every green herb for food"; and it was so. ³¹ Then God saw every-thing that He had made, and indeed *it was* very good. So the evening and the morning were the sixth day.

2 Thus the heavens and the earth, and all the host of them, were fin-ished. ² And on the seventh day God ended His work which He had done, and He rested on the seventh day from all His work which He had done. ³ Then God blessed the seventh day and sanctified it, because in it He rested from all His work which God had created and made.

⁴ This *is* the [a]history of the heavens and the earth when they were created, in the day that the LORD God made the earth and the heavens, ⁵ before any plant of the field was in the earth and before any herb of the field had grown. For the LORD God had not caused it to rain on the earth, and *there was* no man to till the ground; ⁶ but a mist went up from the earth and wa-tered the whole face of the ground.

The difference between prose and poetry is not always so easily distin-guished. Not all poems are written in lines; not all poetry rhymes or uses startling metaphors. And not all prose is without poetic effects. So then how can you tell what a poem is? The simple answer is that you can't. The more complex answer is: it's obvious.

I once provoked some serious concern from a very religious woman when I proclaimed during a lecture that Jesus was a poet. For some odd reason, she did not like that image of Him. Perhaps she thought of poets as socialist, wine-drinking, homeless wanderers spouting bizarre verses of wisdom that contradict an officially recognized view of God and beauty. Maybe she thought of poets as people who hang out with a wide range of unseemly types. Why then, yes: I still maintain that Jesus was a poet. You would be hard pressed to prove otherwise after reading the first chapter of John's Gospel in which we see He is the very Word that creates the world. But before John wrote his book which begins, "In the beginning...," we know of another book that began this way. John obviously knew he was repeating the first verse of the creation story from Genesis to tell his own gospel story, marking a new beginning for mankind. As well, Jesus's concision in telling stories through parables is highly poetic and His sayings such as the Beatitudes are just, flat out, poems in and of themselves. The metaphor is as essential to a poet as a hammer to a builder, and Jesus's passion for the metaphor is undeniable in the way He repeatedly offers a new way of seeing the kingdom of heaven. We know He quotes poetry often, including the Psalms and Isaiah, as he goes about sharing His good news.

There are many definitions of poetry. This is because poetry is indefinable. No one designation will suffice. And we, as intelligent human beings, can't let that go. With each introductory poetry course that I teach, I provide a handout of various famous definitions of it. Here are a few of my favorites:

- Language under pressure. —Adrienne Rich
- Poetry is what gets lost in translation. —Frost
- Poetry is what is found in translation. —Octavio Paz
- Of our conflicts with others we make rhetoric; of our conflicts with ourselves we make poetry. —Yeats
- Poetry is...not life lived but life framed and identified. —R.P. Blackmur
- Poetry is life distilled. —Gwendolyn Brooks
- A language machine. —Donald Hall
- Poetry is the spontaneous overflow of powerful feelings; it takes its origin from emotion recollected in tranquility. —Wordsworth
- Ghostlier demarcations, keener sounds. —Stevens
- The best words in the best order. —Coleridge
- The crown of literature is poetry. It is its end aim. It is the sublimest activity of the human mind. It is the achievement of beauty and delicacy. The writer of prose can only step aside when the poet passes. — W. Somerset Maugham
- I could no more define poetry than a terrier can define a rat. —Housman

I especially like to share the Maugham quote with novelists. Definitions like this, of poetry by poets and writers, are almost endless. I would argue that we are still in the Romantic age when it comes to poetry, because most of my beginning students gravitate toward Wordsworth's emotional definition above, though even he tempers his own romantic view by that last phrase "recollected in tranquility." I tend toward the colder, more mathematical statement by Donald Hall who calls poetry "a language machine." I love to get under the hood of the poem and see how it runs. But I also love Adrienne Rich's very vague definition, "Language under pressure," because it is always useful for students to think about the myriad ways they, as poets or readers, can find the various pressures that make diamonds from the coal of language or maybe the pressure of air worked by hand into a beautiful loaf of bread. Metaphors abound.

But my own definition I try to impress upon readers is this: *Poetry is the language of repetition with variation.* The prime example of repetition with variation in poetry is rhyme, but one can also see this trait in metaphor, allusion, chiasmus, anaphora, and so many other features essential to poetry. We humans like repetition. It provides us with the comfort of recognition and pattern, that the world is not chaotic but ordered. Yet repetition without change quickly becomes monotonous, if not hypnotic to the point of sleep.

As I take a look at the beginning of Genesis, I don't pretend to bring any new revelation to the reading of these amazing words except to show in my own way that it is a kind of poetry. I intend to look at this first chapter (and the first few verses of chapter 2) as a poem, in order to partake of an aesthetic, or beautiful, reading: not just as instructions for life or understanding of living—but for pleasure. Speaking of beginnings: the very beginning of the Westminster Shorter Catechism states that "Man's chief end is to glorify God, and to enjoy Him forever." This enjoyment is the pleasure at which I ultimately aim.

***

Though written in prose, the first chapter of the book of Genesis is rife with repetition. In this first chapter (no coincidence) of my book about poems of deep spiritual meaning, I'd like to highlight some of these repetitions with variation and make an argument about how they function to please the reader. Genesis 1 tells of the creation of the world. It is not a prose instruction manual, rather it is more akin to the way a poem works. For the sake of brevity, I won't go into how the Hebrew language works here. First, I am ill-equipped to show how a language in which I am not fluent makes poetry through its sound, grammar, and syntax. Mostly, for our purposes, I will stick with the English and hopefully show how poetry transcends the difference of languages. As noted above, Frost wrote that "poetry is what gets lost in translation." Still, if you study the Hebrew version of this first chapter of Genesis, you will find Octavio Paz's statement to be true: "Poetry is what is found in translation."

Perhaps it is a good reminder to recognize that the chapter and verse designation is an artificial one put there by scholars of the Word to help us easily locate passages and organize our thoughts. In the initial writing of the book of Genesis, there were no such demarcations. Neither are there numbers of chapters or verses in the letters Paul wrote to his brothers in the faith. But these numbers are obviously helpful in organizing the language into understandable chunks.

It has often been claimed that poetry is about two things: love and death. I believe that poetry is just as often about poetry itself. Poetry is language that looks at itself in the mirror, but that is another argument altogether that deserves a chapter (or book) to itself. But why love and death? My answer: these are the two great mysteries. If the law of nature is "survival of the fittest," why would someone put another's life before one's own (love)? What happens after we finally stop breathing (death)? Neither of these questions are answerable without a great deal of guesswork and philosophies, or faith. So poetry, with its multiplicity of answers and trajectories and possibilities seems a perfect mode of expression to come to terms with these mysteries.

With a poem, there is rarely an answer to anything. And this is why most practical people quickly become frustrated with a poem. They want a meaning, and there is no meaning; there is a multiplicity of meaning. There is a fairly straightforward meaning to a birth announcement or an obituary or a mathematical equation. A great poem continues to offer up meaning after meaning after meaning. Isn't this obvious in the way we can keep coming back to scripture, uncovering new revelations each time, or even the way scholars return to great poems, seeing something fresh and new even though the poem has been critiqued a thousand times?

In Genesis, we begin with a great mystery, or several of them. How can something come from nothing? Where did God come from? What is the nature of God? What is nature? How can time start, and what was before time? These questions are unanswerable, yet Genesis answers these things in the writer's own way, and with multiplicity. However, we don't even know who wrote this. Many believe Moses received the Word directly from God, some believe Moses cobbled together a lot of other stories, and still some others believe a slew of writers developed Genesis over a great period of time. We will probably never know, but scholars make their best guesses upon all the evidence they can find. However, ultimately, human authorship is not as important as whether the words are true or good or even beautiful.

Immediately, the world is divided in twos: heavens and earth, time and timelessness, God and creation, Spirit and flesh, light and dark, form and formlessness, evening and morning, water and air, water and earth, vegetable and animal, animal and man, male and female, mankind and God. These are not all opposites, and many are reflections of the other. In other words, they are repetitions with variations. A few examples, then: an artichoke can seem like a pangolin, the prairies of the Southern plains can seem like a vast sea, the light of evening can seem like the light at dawn, the moon imitates the sun, the jet stream moves like a river, and chapter 2 of Genesis will give a second creation story (not contradictory, but more detailed) showing that the woman is literally, physically, genetically, derived from man. There are repetitions with variations around us all the time, and they are here from the beginning of creation. It pleases us to notice them. Why? Because singularity is not all it's cracked up to be. "It is not good that man should be alone," God says when he gives Eve to Adam. But let's stick to the "poem" of chapter 1 before we go too far afield.

Even God's own person from the beginning is revealed to us as multiple, each part in community with the other, and extending that community to us, created in His image. Of course, you can already see how the repetition (with variation) of the creation story in chapter 2, starting in verse 7, makes this work of literature even more poetic. For our purposes of considering this a poem, let's say our poem goes from Genesis 1:1 through 2:6, and let's say the second creation story (its own poem?) begins with 2:7.

God commands male and female to be creative, and we realize that not only can God create man, but men and women will then mirror God in creating mankind. The scripture tells us that God blesses them and gives them their first command, to be creative: "Be fruitful and multiply." Of course, that fruitfulness need not only have to do with the procreation of children, but also with every other task to which we set our hearts, minds, and bodies. As a poet and short story writer, I immediately think of how God sets story and song into motion to create the world through words. Then, being made in God's image, am I not capable of doing the same? Not exactly. I can't create a physical horse by saying "horse," but I can certainly create an imaginative one you can believe in if I write the poem or story well enough. If God is first and foremost a Creator and I am made in his image, I ought to fulfill my first calling to be a creator. All humans have this calling upon them to be creative and imaginative in some fruitful and fulfilling way. Notice the word *image* is the root of *imaginative*. Some words are so obvious we often forget their origins. That is what poetry demands; it asks us to pay attention to *how* language is working, and not just *what* it means.

Ask yourself what other kinds of repetitions with variation are happening in this supposed poem. Obviously, we have the repetition of days, and "the evening and the morning" are the limits of these days. And we have the repetition of the nights. Each morning has a dawn, and each evening the sun sets, yet there is a difference in each day. The other obvious repetition in each day of creation is that "God saw that it was good." Six days God creates and without fail, without variation, he sees that it is good. And then the seventh day varies still more than the others. The sun still rises and sets, but God rests and enjoys the goodness of his creation.

The regularity through repetition of the syntax as the days of creation move forward provides the world with a reliable order. Each day, "God said"… "let there be"… "and it was so"… and "it was good." Surely, we can relate to this orderliness of things in our lives and our desire for how our future proceeds. Breakfast, work/school, lunch, work/school, dinner, rest, sleep. No one can deny that such a routine brings comfort. And cause and effect are established. If God speaks His will, it happens, and it is good. Of course, no variation from this routine would bring monotony and boredom.

Genesis 1:26 is one of my favorite verses in the Bible. If we believe it, this verse is the foundation of all we believe or think, and it should affect our worldview and behavior. First of all, there is the extraordinary mystery of the plural God who is invoked when the first person plural is used.

Thrice! "Let *Us* make man in *Our* image" it says (italics mine), "according to *Our* likeness. Let them have dominion..." There are many explanations for this strange use of the pronoun, including the use of the royal "We." Obviously, Christians see this three-personed God as Father, Son, and Holy Spirit. We still see God as the One true God, but in three manifestations. No theologian would argue that this should be simply understood, and many would admit it is downright confounding such that one must take it by faith. The Muslim criticizes it as heresy; as for them there is only one God, and this theological math does not add up. Still, it is not impossible to see that I, myself, am a father, a son, and a spirit (not in the same way that God is, as I am created and He is not). Sigmund Freud's theory of psychology argues that I am an id, ego, and superego: different aspects of one being. I wonder where Freud got this idea for such a wonderful complexity?

This being-created-in-God's-image, one of the greatest revelations of the entire Bible, reveals that we are set apart from the rest of creation. The poet William Blake famously and wildly claimed that "Every thing that lives is holy." But scripture makes it clear that each person has a special relationship with God. We alone are made in His image, and our unique position in the created world is that we are to have dominion over all other living things. I probably need not point out that dominion is not the same as domination or abuse or waste, and that good stewardship and caretaking are at the heart of being a good servant. However, in our present day and age, the destruction of earth and atmosphere, of flora and fauna, by man is at an all-time high. Or should I say low? Nevertheless, there is a huge movement of evangelicals led by thinkers such as Christian climate scientist Katharine Hayhoe (one of my esteemed colleagues at Texas Tech University) who deeply understand our complex relationship with the rest of creation and what we can do to take care of it, even as Adam was instructed to take care of his own Paradise. And certainly, God gave him his limitations: Leave that tree over there alone.

Still, what does it mean to be made in God's image? Well, for one, we see that though we are not begotten of God like Jesus, we can be adopted into the family of God with full rights as children of God, inheriting all good things. This can be a selfish perspective, no doubt...until we see that all other men and women are made in this image and that our morals now stem from this core principle of Judeo-Christian ontology: our being, each one of us, should reflect the nature of God. When we bless or curse, help or harm, lift up or strike down, educate or deceive another person, we are doing it toward the very image of God. By this standard we are able to determine that man is not the measure of all, but there is a primacy beyond us, above us. It makes perfect sense when Jesus tells us (twice) in a parable in Matthew 25: "inasmuch as you did it (or not) to one of the least of these, My brethren, you did it to Me." Our actions and inactions toward one another are inseparable from our relationship with God. We cannot so easily separate out our secular poems from our sacred ones. For the Christian, all poems are for Him.

The apostle Paul argues in Ephesians 2:10 that we are God's workmanship. As I mentioned in the introduction, the word in the Greek is *poeima*. When I look at twenty of the most common Bible translations I see this word as *creation, handiwork, masterpiece,* and *creatures,* though not a single one translates *poeima* as *poem.* Odd, no? Nevertheless, are we not God's poem? That idea fits well with the idea of a poem as a language machine. Are we not every day of our lives language machines, using our songs, stories, arguments, phone calls, texts, whispers and rants, to transport ourselves and our missions? Are we not a special creation in that we think and understand the world through our use of words? But more than the linguistic aspect of who we are, we are created by a poet who knows a little something about order and beauty. If, as Coleridge said, poems are the best words in the best order, then we have a promising potential.

This first poem, as I am picturing it, of Genesis 1 and 2, this creation story, begins and ends with the same phrasing, but arranged into a beautiful chiasmus at the end. We go from: "In the beginning, God created the heavens and the earth" to "This is the history of the heavens and the earth when they were created, in the day that the Lord God made the earth and the heavens." Notice how the chiasmus works: from "heavens…earth…created" to a conclusion of the Lord who "made…earth…heavens."

Also, the final repetition with variation here is the very name of God. We develop from God to Lord God—in the Hebrew, from Elohim to Yawheh-Elohim. At first introduction, our Creator is referred to with a name that we take to indicate his power and authority. Then, after the creation of man in His own image, God is no longer just a creator but now in a personal relationship, so He has a name, not just a title. A name allows us to draw close to someone and provides us with familiarity.

As the greater epic of all Scripture, the Bible, unfolds, we'll see God's name continue to be repeated in beautiful variation. And isn't this the greatest set of "rhymes" for all believers? To have at the ready the many names of God: Creator, Lord, Father, Son, Holy Spirit, Counselor, Almighty, Healer, Comforter, Provider, Master, I Am, Love…

***

The first actual poem in the Bible is just a few verses down the page beginning in Genesis 2:23 after God performs divine surgery upon Adam to create Eve. What can Adam do when he sees her but write the first poem, a love poem?

And Adam said:

This is now bone of my bones
And flesh of my flesh;
She shall be called Woman,
Because she was taken out of Man.

The scripture shows us that Adam had to name with ordered words the beautiful creation before him. We see in the poem this obvious repetition with variation in the way that *Woman* rhymes with *Man*. The Hebrew is *Ishah* (woman) and *Ish* (man). The combination here is not only the repetition-variation of the sound of the words but also the repetition of the flesh, of the bone, all the way down to the chromosomes which are similar but varied (XY and XX). Then, Moses's conclusion of chapter 2 following Adam's poem acts as yet another chiasmus with the husband being joined to the wife, becoming one flesh. It would not be long before the coupling of these two would create yet another rhyme, children, who would carry forward the action of the poem through time, through failure, toward a second Adam, who will, so we believe, restore Paradise. It is fitting, then, that Jesus, as poet, in the mortal image of his immortal form, tells us we "must be born again."

Between Heaven and Earth:
Christian Wiman's "Dust Devil":

Dust Devil

Mystical hysterical amalgam of earth and wind
and mind

over and of
the much-loved

dust you go
through a field I know

by broken heart
for I have learned this art

of flourishing
vanishing

wherein to live
is to move

cohesion
illusion

wild untouchable toy
called by a boy

God's top
in a time when time stopped.

Once readers know of Christian Wiman's medical condition, many may see his poems only through the lens of death and dying: for many years, he has been living with a serious blood disease (and he was raised in West Texas, another mortal wound). If you read his wonderful essays in both of his prose collections, you come to understand the gravity and grace of his personal history, family troubles, and his physical suffering. The prose is beautiful, stylistically some of the best essays about poetry I have ever read. Especially in *Ambition and Survival: Becoming a Poet,* a reader comes to understand Wiman's early journey into and through the world of poetry. He grows up in windy, lonely West Texas, escaping to college in the East. Not satisfied to take an ordinary path, he travels abroad and on various expeditions that will eventually lead him to the heights of our contemporary Parnassus as editor of *Poetry Magazine,* where he dramatically changes the famous journal which had become stagnant and dull with the slight, free-verse, meditative poems of the seventies and eighties.

I know from personal experience that, serving as a poetry editor, one's own creative work often diminishes as others are supported, encouraged and championed. Editorial work is one of constant self-sacrifice. From his book we learn that, for a number of years, Wiman stops writing poems. Yet, when he falls sick and gets his diagnosis, having recently fallen in love, despite the fact that he should be less capable than ever to produce a poem, he begins to write verse again with renewed power. With a wilder, more dense texture of words and play of syntax than his first two poetry collections, Wiman's poems tackle head-on his disease and his world with what Wallace Stevens calls "ghostlier demarcations, keener sounds."

However, if a poem is to succeed, it needs to achieve that success not only in the person of the poet but in the realm of the reader and beyond that into the territory of the English language. The poet needs to connect with us on multiple levels: through not only personal suffering but with the way we speak and how we live in the world both bound by Time and freed by the imagination.

A young boy by the name of Mattie Stepanek took the publishing world by storm some years back, writing emotionally moving poems about his fight with muscular dystrophy and the imaginative strength it took for him to endure an awful disease in his very short life (he died when he was only fourteen). However, while his poems might move some to tears, they don't rise to the height of literature where the language stands alone beyond the life. And death. I don't mean to diminish Stepanek's achievement, but any careful reader can see his verse does not rise to what a masterful poet does with lines. I cringe at my own ungenerous criticism because poetry is partly about emotional feeling. But in a great poem, the language of verse has to do more. Language should become new to us or, in other words, as the great Russian formalist critic Viktor Shklovsky expressed it: *defamiliarized*. Great poems never give us what we expect; they give us what we never expected. When we think of *defamiliarization*, we might think of its root word, *family*, and how a prodigal son returned home might, because of his loss and return, come back to become more of a son than he ever was back when all seemed comfortable and, yes, familiar.

This is why cliché is the antithesis of poetry. Once in a poetry class I was teaching, a student felt the need to defend his overuse of cliché in the poems he was writing. "I like cliché," he said to me and to the class. I said that, well, yes, we all like clichés; that is why we use them so much. But clichés are the opposite of poetry. Clichés are made of overused language that wants us to forget the vibrant possibilities of a word or words. They leave us with a general sense of things that, because of overuse and familiarity, quickly gets the job done in communicating a notion. Poetry, instead, draws our attention to words, not just feelings or ideas. Poetry complicates words so they point in different directions, creating possibilities, whereas cliché simplifies. Poetry is not just about a writer and a reader coming together; poetry connects humanity to *how* we say words, exposing their vulnerabilities and strengths. Poetry works. I like lying around on the couch sometimes, but there's more to life.

A poem is always a multiplicity of meanings suspended in a beautiful balance, and this is why we read and re-read the great poems. They keep offering up new readings, new possibilities, and as a result they show us the heights and depths of our experience. I believe that books of poetry should be generally of more literary value than fiction because you get much more use out of them. Very few books of fiction are worth coming back to on a regular basis. Obviously, those novels we do reread are considered "poetic." But poetry, of its own nature, has within itself the quality of repetition.

Without a doubt, part of my own reaction (mostly delight) to Christian Wiman's West Texas poems is affected by having lived near the poet's early stomping grounds. The mesquite, the miles of cotton, the pumpjacks, the brutal sun (here, we understand the reason for cowboy hats), the open fields and open sky, the dust devils—these are all part of my life now. I identify with the flatland flora, fauna, the hundreds of miles of farmland, and the unique place that Wiman sees and names.

When I first moved to Texas nearly twenty years ago, I was unloading some cans and bottles from my car in a recycling center parking lot when a dust devil struck me unaware. I closed my eyes and ducked my head into my armpit. Five seconds later the entire car's black interior, along with my hair and all my clothing, was filled with ten thousand pieces of straw and as many chunks of dirt, trash, and sand. I intimately know what a dust devil is, for it took me the rest of the afternoon to clean the car. It happened once again when I was teaching a poetry class in Junction, Texas, almost ripping the roof off the pavilion where my class and I were sheltered from the sun…but not the wind. We could see it coming across the field toward us, swirling its dust and dead grass, and we thought it would veer away, but no. It was upon us, and we all buried our heads beneath our hands on the picnic table where we were seated. We held onto what we could. A few seconds later, in the calm after the storm, wiping the dust from our eyes and the grass and dirt from our hair, we got up to retrieve our poems and pens and pencils that were scattered all around us. We all had a good laugh at our unique Texas experience.

However, a connection with Wiman's locale isn't why I love to reread his poems. There are plenty of bad poems written about the heroics of the Alamo or the beauty of our wide open spaces of bluebonnet-bespattered Texas. I love Wiman's poems because the poems themselves love the sound and shape of language. The first poem in the book, "Dust Devil" is a masterwork of form and function, not only because we connect with the speaker's vision of the world and personal pain, but primarily because the poem renews our faith in language and an understanding of our mortal condition in the very presence of God.

The poem is not an epiphany or a set of directions, but an ordering of whirling words that penetrate our existence and move beyond our lives toward…what? What is that dust devil? The sum of its parts? The chaotic world of our lives? God? The Devil? Death? Time? Memory? Poetry? Suffering? Well, yes, all of these, depending on where you are in the poem and how you are reading it. Such a short poem, and such power. In the way God might speak out of the wind to a suffering man, one is reminded of one of the oldest poems, the Book of Job.

To read this poem is to be struck by a dust devil. Wiman gives us, pictorially, a vision of the phenomenon itself, a vertical line of continuous words touching earth and sky (note the longer first and last lines which express these limits). The words swirl down the page through the use of one thin stanza of short lines to touch finally the end of the time of the poem, the end of the spinning of this mini-tornado of a sentence. The poem begins with an allusion to one of the most famous poems of the 20th Century, Allen Ginsberg's "Howl." That poem's first line reads: "I saw the best minds of my generation destroyed by madness, starving hysterical naked." Wiman says in the first two lines something quite similar: "Mystical hysterical amalgam of earth and wind / and mind."

Both poets begin their first lines with the words "hysterical" and "mind" and a mystically-charged long sentence (Wiman's entire poem is one sentence, and Ginsberg's entire first section of "Howl" is a ridiculously long rant of a sentence) to create an atmosphere of wildness in the chaotic and grieving mind of the speaker. The word "hysterical" means "of the womb" and etymologically signifies the frantic feelings of separation between a woman and her child. For Ginsberg, these feelings were brought on by the death of his friends, habitual drug abuse, and an upheaval in the political climate of the fifties stemming from the abuses of patriarchal, capitalist power. For Wiman, the hysterical seems to be the evocation of a childhood memory stemming from this meditation on a dust devil. He is trying to get back to that childhood self through his memory of what a dust devil must have been like for him then. Like crawling back into the womb, the reaching for this memory hints at being born again. Both poems clearly aim at a deeper look into a spiritual realm. Ginsberg uses the word "angel" eight times in the first section of his poem. Whereas Ginsberg sustains the litany of his poem through the use of anaphora, repeating "who" a few dozen times at the beginnings of lines to sustain his rant, Wiman's repetitions are slant and standard rhymes at the ends of the lines. Ginsberg's lines are very long, and Wiman's couldn't be much shorter. In one couplet of "Dust Devil," there are only two words: "cohesion / illusion."

In another couplet, Wiman uses what might seem like a cliché: "by broken heart." A close reader realizes that the broken heart here is not hurt feelings but the brokenness of the way we know things "by heart," or through memory. Wiman is recollecting his childhood in lines which *break*, or turn back on themselves in what we call verse. It is arguable that where a poet breaks a line is more important than any other choice he can make in writing a poem. It is the one definite maneuver that distinguishes poetry from prose. And yet, the broken words are forced into rhyming couplets by the poet, reuniting the words back together in a different way. This broken heart is, as well, the poet's own removal from his childhood where he might have lived more innocently. In Wiman's case, in a way, it is a physically broken heart that is pumping cancerous blood throughout his body. As you can see, this is no cliché. The cliché of a "broken heart" has been redeemed back into the land of valuable language. It is literally "interesting," as its value grows its investment in the poem.

One of the most important aspects of the poem is its identification of a dust devil as a phenomenon that is both a coherent thing and yet an illusion, a trick of light. It may very well look like a solid entity, like a cloud, but it is made up of mostly air. If it ceases to spin, it disappears. If you have ever witnessed this meteorological event, you have noticed that as it moves across a field it picks up more debris and dust and builds, and then it dies down, and then it builds again, fluctuating in a somewhat random manner. The poem notices this dual nature of the dust devil. There one minute, but not there the next. Like God, perhaps.

Ultimately, what does the dust devil represent? An inept English teacher might ask this of his students, as if there is one ultimate representation. In fact, across America one hears teachers all the time demand of students some kind of answer to a poem's meaning. In the film *Splendor in the Grass*, in the famous classroom scene, Deanie Loomis' teacher demands of her "what the poet means." Her character has other issues, for sure, but, unable to answer the question, no wonder she runs out from the classroom in tears! She couldn't possibly answer the question correctly to satisfy both herself and the teacher. There isn't a correct answer!

A good reader of a poem understands that the dust devil represents, complicatedly, the poem in not only its shape, but how words are untouchable, coherent, momentary, and illusory. The dust devil is also indicative of how in our lives we remember things, in fits and starts. Also, it evokes the

31

nature of God, as nearly invisible yet incarnate and powerful, of course, in the same way. But it is a "devil," and this complicates the reading, doesn't it? Jesus was called a devil by the Pharisees. And in the garden, the devil tells us that we can be like God. At the end of the poem, the subject isn't God or the Devil, rather it is "God's top," a "toy," which takes us to Kafka's philosopher who believes he could understand the world if he could just understand, via synecdoche, in one moment of stillness, a child's spinning top. There's the problem. You stop it, and it no longer is what it is. As Wiman says in this poem, "to live / is to move." This is reminiscent of Paul who says, "In Him we live and move and have our being, as also some of your own poets have said" (Acts 17:28). Just like a poem, movement is necessary to a person, or God. Life requires motion and the power of the spirit. The blood, and its spiraling DNA within, must circulate through the body and regenerate with renewed oxygen.

And a top is not only a toy. It means *height*. What is God's top, His height? It is both infinite and, in the Christian worldview, maybe around six feet high, on the move, short-lived, through the deserts of the Middle East a couple thousand years ago. The couplets rhyme evenly and unevenly throughout, cohering and blurring. In the poem, we have earth, air, and fire (the moving "mind" of the poem), but no water: remember we're in a very arid West Texas where water is scarce.

As with so many great poems, this is an *ars poetica*, a poem about poetry itself, and its unwillingness to be simply one thing or defined in any final way. Perhaps what is most astonishing is that Christian Wiman, editor of *Poetry Magazine* when he wrote this poem, surrounded perhaps more than anybody by the cacophony of American poetry, has an ear for silence. Here and in so many of his other recent poems, he presses his ear against the hive of belief. It takes a renewed child-like faith, and Wiman achieves a kind of certainty through memory and imagination and, one might suppose, grace. You get for a moment the feeling at the end of the poem that "time stopped" is the victory of the grave. But all one need do is begin the poem again to ask "death, where is thy sting?" A good poem is never over when it's over. A poem this good bears re-reading.

In another poem appearing later in *Every Riven Thing*, Christian Wiman's Southwestern landscape reveals to him that "to believe is to believe you have been torn / from the abyss, yet stand waveringly on its rim." In the twenty-first century, one usually cringes when a poet uses the term "abyss," but with this use of the actual landscape, a canyon, the term is earned. In West Texas, we don't have mountains, rather we have canyons, depressions that seemingly out of nowhere open up beneath our feet. The dramatic variation of the landscape that takes our breath away slopes downward. Wiman's belief here does not emanate from an easy or unexamined vision. It is a salvation from the pit of death. At the heart of his poems made of dust and howling wind is the demanding gravity of the hope of resurrection, and a sustained belief in the evidence of things not seen, yet seen through poetry.

To See to See:
Emily Dickinson's "I heard a Fly buzz"

I heard a Fly buzz - when I died - (591)

I heard a Fly buzz — when I died —
The Stillness in the Room
Was like the Stillness in the Air —
Between the Heaves of Storm —

The Eyes around — had wrung them dry —
And Breaths were gathering firm
For that last Onset — when the King
Be witnessed — in the Room —

I willed my Keepsakes — Signed away
What portion of me be
Assignable — and then it was
There interposed a Fly —

With Blue — uncertain — stumbling Buzz —
Between the light — and me —
And then the Windows failed — and then
I could not see to see —

What happens when we die? I asked this to a senior level poetry class a few years ago. We were talking about a poem that was contemplating the mystery of death. I can't remember the poem, as probably half the poems worth reading are about death.

The class of eleven students sat there, refusing to answer. Come on, I said, give me an answer or your best guess. You don't have to be right, I told them. None of us really knows. At least not in the way we know other things of this world. A few of them groaned, confessing they didn't want to get into a religious discussion. Finally, one student said, "Nothing. Nothing happens. You die, and that's it." A few of the others agreed with him. I didn't count, but it was about half the class believing that after death there would be nothing. One of those students said probably your energy went back into the universe, but when I asked her how she knew or what that meant, she couldn't answer. She just felt it. One student said she believed you went to heaven or hell, and she said it was something that she just took by faith. The rest seemed terrified.

I tried to put them at ease and told them I promised I wasn't grading them on their answers. We're in college, and this is a great place to have these kinds of conversations, thinking for yourself. I just wanted to know what they thought, and it directly had to do with the poem we were reading. I stated (and many of them probably knew from previous conversations) that I was a Christian believer, so I believed in second life, though I admitted it's a great mystery. I quoted the book of Hebrews: "It is appointed unto man once to die, and then the judgment." I said that my belief in second life informs my life here and now. The student who was a self-avowed atheist opened up and took it further, perhaps to challenge me. He said that he lived his life for himself, for the greatest pleasure, day by day, because in the end, all you know is yourself, and it just ends. I joked and said I felt sorry for his girlfriend. We all had a good laugh at that, though his laugh was a little more nervous than the others.

My point in telling this story is that I think this conversation brought out into the open a relationship between how we see death and how we live a life of love. The student arguing with me might have as easily believed that he achieved the most pleasure out of loving his girlfriend, of sacrificing for her, but instead, he could hardly admit she existed. Everything could be an illusion, he claimed. Except for the fact that he, himself, exists. Since it wasn't a philosophy class, and the students were visibly uncomfortable, we moved back to the poem at hand, but I was a little shocked that in a university in a place as conservative as West Texas, so many of the students would embrace or even tolerate such nihilism.

Great poems, though, do often tackle death head on. Emily Dickinson, one of our first great American poets, wrote many poems on the theme of death. One of the most striking and most anthologized is "I heard a Fly buzz." Dickinson didn't title most of her poems, so we often use the first phrase or line of her poem as a title. In her poetry, she was idiosyncratic in many ways, though in others very tied to tradition. Her use of dashes instead of regular punctuation is a hallmark of the individuality of her poetry. She often deals in big abstractions and capitalizes odd words here and there with seemingly no set pattern or method of doing this. She loved to rhyme, and perhaps more than anything else is famous for her slant or near rhymes. Another of her more famous poems begins: "Tell all the truth but tell it slant—"

One of the traditional aspects many of her poems exhibit is a use of the ballad form (or an approximation of it). This form uses the iambic meter in a fairly regular rhythm to emphasize a 4/3/4/3 pattern in its stanzas. Sometimes this alternates to a 3/4/3/4 or something in between. Here is a slightly earlier example of this form:

Amazing grace. How sweet the sound
that saved a wretch like me.
I once was lost, but now am found.
Was blind, but now I see.

John Newton's hymn may be the most popular tune in the English speaking world. President Obama famously sang it at the funeral of Clementa Pinckney shortly after the mass-murder of African-Americans in Charleston back in 2015. The regular meter and rhyme of the 4/3/4/3 stanzas create a very tidy formal boundary, and with that an easy way to remember the words.

The Great Awakening in England and the revival that followed in America was spread, in part, by some of the church leaders' capacity for writing songs in this ballad form that we also refer to as common hymn quatrain. John and Charles Wesley were two of the more prolific hymn writers. Charles himself wrote more than six thousand. Of course, the music of the hymn quatrain is open to different arrangements even though the meter of the words is strictly metrical. For instance, consider how rhythmically different the song "Amazing Grace" is from the song "A Mighty Fortress is our God." I like to point out to students that this ballad form continues to be used in a wide range of songs. From "The Theme to

Gilligan's Island" to "Sweet Child O' Mine" by Guns N' Roses to a recent murder ballad by Jason Isbell called "Live Oak," this rhythmical setup continues to offer a useful pattern for musicians to create new tunes.

***

Many think of Emily Dickinson as an odd eccentric woman who wore white dresses and rarely came out of her room. While that might well describe her later years, when she was younger she had quite a normal upper-class upbringing. She even went to college. Prior to and during her time at Mount Holyoke there was a Christian revival spreading throughout New England, and although it seems she wanted to be a part of it, something within her couldn't surrender. In a letter to her childhood friend, Abiah Root, in early 1846, she bares her feelings frankly:

Dear Abiah.

I fear you have thought me very long in answering your affectionate letter and especially considering the circumstances under which you wrote. But I am sure if you could have looked in upon me Dear A. since I received your letter you would heartily forgive me for my long delay.

I was delighted to receive an answer to my own so soon. Under any other circumstances I should have answered your letter sooner. But I feared lest in the unsettled state of your mind in regard to which choice you should make, I might say something which might turn your attention from so all important a subject. I shed many tears over your letter — the last part of it. I hoped and still I feared for you. I have had the same feelings myself Dear A. I was almost persuaded to be a christian. I thought I never again could be thoughtless and worldly - and I can say that I never enjoyed such perfect peace and happiness as the short time in which I felt I had found my savior. But I soon forgot my morning prayer or else it was irksome to me. One by one my old habits returned and I cared less for religion than ever. I have longed to hear from you - to know what decision you have made. I hope you are a christian for I feel that it is impossible for any one to be happy without a treasure in heaven. I feel that I shall never be happy without

I love Christ.

When I am most happy there is a sting in every enjoyment. I find no rose without a thorn. There is an aching void in my heart which I am convinced the world never can fill. I am far from being thoughtless upon the subject of religion. I continually hear Christ saying to me Daughter give me thine heart. Probably you have made your decision long before this time. Perhaps you have exchanged the fleeting pleasures of time for a crown of immortality. Perhaps the shining company above have tuned their golden harps to the song of one more redeemed sinner. I hope at sometime the heavenly gates will be opened to receive me and The angels will consent to call me sister. I am continually putting off becoming a christian. Evil voices lisp in my ear — There is yet time enough. I feel that every day I live I sin more and more in closing my heart to the offers of mercy which are presented to me freely — Last winter there was a revival here. The meetings were thronged by people old and young. It seemed as if those who sneered loudest at serious things were soonest brought to see their power, and to make Christ their portion. It was really wonderful to see how near heaven came to sinful mortals. Many who felt there was nothing in religion determined to go once & see if there was anything in it, and they were melted at once.

Perhaps you will not believe it Dear A. but I attended none of the meetings last winter. I felt that I was so easily excited that I might again be deceived and I dared not trust myself. Many conversed with me seriously and affectionately and I was almost inclined to yield to the claims of He who is greater than I. How ungrateful I am to live along day by day upon Christ's bounty and still be in a state of enmity to him & his cause.

Does not Eternity appear dreadful to you. I often get thinking of it and it seems so dark to me that I almost wish there was no Eternity. To think that we must forever live and never cease to be. It seems as if Death which all so dread because it launches us upon an unknown world would be a relief to so endless a state of existence. I don't know why it is but it does not seem to me that I shall ever cease to live on earth - I cannot imagine with the farthest stretch of my imagination my own death scene - It does not seem to me that I shall ever close my eyes in death. I cannot realize that the grave will be my last home - that friends will weep over my coffin and that my name will be mentioned, as one who has ceased to be among the haunts of the living, and it will be wondered where my disembodied spirit has flown. I cannot realize that the friends I have seen pass from my sight in the prime of their days like dew before the sun will not again walk the streets and act their parts in the great drama of life, nor can I realize that when I again meet them it will be in another & a far different world from this. I hope we shall all be acquitted at the bar of God, and shall receive the welcome, Well done Good & faithful Servants., Enter Ye into the Joy of your Lord. I wonder if we shall know each other in heaven, and whether we shall be a chosen band as we are here. I am inclined to believe that we shall - and that our love will be purer in heaven than on earth. I feel that life is short and time fleeting - and that I ought now to make my peace with my maker - I hope the golden opportunity is not far hence when my heart will willingly yield itself to Christ, and that my sins will be all blotted out of the book of remembrance.

Another letter in late March 1846 reveals more of her state of mind and heart, recognizing that her friend has made a profession of faith:

Dearest Abiah

It is Sabbath Eve. All is still around me & I feel in a mood to answer your affectionate letter. I am alone before my little writing desk, & wishing I could write news to you as joyful as your letter to me contained. I am alone with God, & my mind is filled with many solemn thoughts which crowd themselves upon me with an irresistible force. I think of Dear Sarah & yourself as the only two out of our circle of five who have found a Saviour. I shed many a tear & gave many a serious thought to your letter & wished that I had found the peace which has been given to you. I had a melancholy pleasure in comparing your present feelings with what mine once were, but are no more. I think of the perfect happiness I experienced while I felt I was an heir of heaven as of a delightful dream, out of which the Evil one bid me wake & again return to the world & its pleasures. Would that I had not listened to his winning words! The few short moments in which I loved my Saviour I would not now exchange for a thousand worlds like this. It was then my greatest pleasure to commune alone with the great God & to feel that he would listen to my prayers. I determined to devote my whole life to his service & desired that all might taste of the stream of living water from which I cooled my thirst. But the world allured me & in an unguarded moment I listened to her syren voice. From that moment I seemed to lose my interest in heavenly things by degrees. Prayer in which I had taken such delight became a task & the small circle who met for prayer missed me from their number. Friends reasoned with me & told me of the danger I was in of grieving away the Holy spirit of God. I felt my danger & was alarmed in view of it, but I had rambled too far to return & ever since my heart has been growing harder & more distant from the truth & now I have bitterly to lament my folly - & also my own indifferent state at the present time.

I feel that I am sailing upon the brink of an awful precipice, from which I cannot escape & over which I fear my tiny boat will soon glide if I do not receive help from above. There is now a revival in College & many hearts have given way to the claims of God. What if it should extend to the village church and your friends A. & E. feel its influence. Would that it might be so.

Although I feel sad that one should be taken and the others left, yet it is with joy that Abby & I peruse your letter & read your decision in favor of Christ & though we are not in the fold yet I hope when the great sheperd at the last day separates the sheep from the goats we may hear his voice & be with the lambs upon the right hand of God. I know that I ought now to give myself away to God & spend the springtime of life in his service for it seems to me a mockery to spend life's summer & autumn in the service of Mammon & when the world no longer charms us, "When our eyes are dull of seeing & our ears of hearing, when the silver cord is loosed & the golden bowl broken" to yield our hearts, because we are afraid to do otherwise & give to God the miserable recompense of a sick bed for all his kindness to us. Surely it is a fearful thing to live & a very fearful thing to die & give up our account to the supreme ruler for all our sinful deeds & thoughts upon this probationary term of existence. I feel when I seriously reflect upon such things as Dr Young when he exclaimed, O! what a miracle to man is man -

Yesterday as I sat by the north window the funeral train entered the open gate of the church yard, following the remains of Judge Dickinson's wife to her long home. His wife has borne a long sickness of two or three years without a murmur. She relied wholly upon the arm of God & he did not forsake her. She is now with the redeemed in heaven & with the savior she has so long loved according to all human probability.

In yet another letter to Abiah in September 1846, Emily describes very clearly her ongoing struggle:

...I feel that I have not yet made my peace with God. I am still a s[tran]ger—to the delightful emotions which fill your heart. I have perfect confidence in God & his promises & yet I know not why, I feel that the world holds a predominant place in my affections. I do not feel I could give up all for Christ, were I called to die. Pray for me Dear A. that I may yet enter into the kingdom, that there may be room left for me in the shining courts above.

From these letters one gets the sense that Dickinson had once made a profession of faith, but now she is under the impression that, if she is to be a true believer, she has to forsake any love of the world whatsoever. This she cannot seem to do, so she remains torn.

Dickinson's poems can be fairly maddening due to their wild ambiguities, but these same ambiguities are also why so many readers love her verse. The big abstractions, strange dashes, wild syntax, and multiplicity of inventions create possibilities of interpretation that vary widely, and no one answer will do for describing any moment in a Dickinson poem. Her spiritual vacillation is very much like her poetic difficulty. She cannot settle for a single answer. As she says in another poem: "I dwell in possibility / a Fairer house than prose." She was a prolific letter writer all her life , and her prose letters regarding faith issues reveal great turmoil, whereas the poetry allows her to make more potentially positive claims. Note that in the above-mentioned phrase, she doesn't say she dwells in poetry, even though this is likely what she means because it is counter to the word prose. Even that maneuver suggests a multiplicity of vision rather than having to decide on one thing.

Dickinson is similar to other important writers of her day in that she ultimately takes a kind of transcendental view of religion. These writers embraced a much more ambiguous interpretation of spiritual things and expected as much from those around them. Conventional religious dogma and doctrine had, for these transcendentalists, become a limited, limiting, and negative way of understanding God and spiritual matters. Like the Romantics before them, they looked to the natural world, to Nature with a capital N, for revelation about who they might be and how they might live in the world. Emerson, Hawthorne, and Thoreau were the most famous prose writers of this school of thought, each working in his own vein. Looking back, we can see that Walt Whitman and Emily Dickinson were the important poets, though they were not recognized much in their own time. And these two were the first *great* American poets. Of course, there had been a good number of Americans writing poetry in her first few hundred years (even Emerson), but Whitman and Dickinson were the first to achieve a mastery of the language in truly unique styles. Appropriate to the American experiment, both of them wrote poems obsessed with freedom. Whitman wrote the poems of freedom *in* the world, and Dickinson wrote the poems of freedom *from* the world.

***

The poem "I heard a Fly buzz" is a strange one that delivers to its reader a direct struggle with belief through a vision of death. It does seem like a vision, but we will see by the end of the poem that this is not exactly the right word. The poem begins with the sense of hearing. But this listening immediately becomes ambiguous due to the "when" of the poem. "I heard…when I died," Dickinson writes. We are in a peculiar state of being, as this is not before or after a death but "when I died." It is a moment no one would be able to hear in the natural world, and a moment made even more bizarre by the fact that a poem is being written after the fact of death.

It gets weirder. What would be the difference between "The Stillness in the Room" vs. "the Stillness in the Air"? And what are these "Heaves of Storm"? How is there a storm when all is still? One detects a kind of spiritual battle going on, perhaps over the soul of the departed. And yet she is speaking.

Next we get a sense of the community who are gathered in the room where our speaker is lying. We observe a moment after grieving. The tears have been cried and the breaths of those attending are now "gathering firm," seemingly composing themselves. But what to make of this "Onset"? An onset is usually the beginning of something negative. Here it is followed by a King being witnessed. And not just "a" king but "the King." One assumes Jesus, the final judge. We should remember the irony of His earthly crown of thorns.

Things seem out of order again, as the speaker at this point "willed her Keepsakes" and leaves some kind of inheritance. But you can't do that after you die; only before. However, with the next few lines re-introducing this buzzing Fly, we see that perhaps time has all been conflated here and, after all, there was a sequence of events that happened leading up to this buzz. Perhaps this strange arrangement of time in the poem can make more sense if we understand that after death, the soul is not bound by earthly time or space—as far as we know.

The fly "interposing" here "With Blue— uncertain — stumbling Buzz" is given a specific location between the speaker and the light. Once that happens "the Windows failed." The "Blue…Buzz" is a wonderful example of synesthesia. One could interpret this to be the fly landing not on actual windows but on the speaker's eyes, blotting out the light. Certain types of flies can detect death quickly, especially the blow fly, which is a blue green color. Forensic entomologists often determine time of death by the presence and number of these flies and/or their larvae on the body of the deceased. The eyes or, as we know them, the "windows of the soul," have "failed," probably because the fly has landed on them in order to gain that opening into the body where she can lay her eggs. In the same way that the Stillnesses between Room and Air were conflated earlier, I believe that the Windows and the eyes here have been unified. In death, space and time collapse. The synesthesia is slightly terrifying, as well, because the "Blue" of the fly ends up blotting out the blue of the sky that might be seen through the window, which is suggestive of heaven. Notice that the Fly has become a Buzz at this point. Blindness has already set in.

The "uncertain stumbling," to any believer, catches the ear. These two words are loaded with connotations of spiritual failure. But we should also understand that the opposite of faith is not doubt: it is certainty. So Dickinson's uncertainty is something any and all of us have encountered in our pursuit of truth or even wisdom. And while the phrase is associated with the fly, one might also connect it to the speaker of the poem, especially because the space between the two has been erased. Has the speaker made a certain profession of faith, or has she been "uncertain"? Has she stumbled in sin in her life? The last line will give us a terrifying suggestion.

As mentioned earlier, one of the most famous hymns of all time is John Newton's "Amazing Grace." Newton had led a dissolute life and even worked in slave trading. A near shipwreck turned his life around spiritually, and at the age of 43 he began preaching and writing hymns. Nearly every English speaking adult in America knows that Newton's final line of the first quatrain reads: "was blind but now I see."

Dickinson, who had grown up in the church, would know these lyrics. She chooses to end her own "hymn": "I could not see to see—," clearly mocking Newton's words. Unlike Newton's repentant singer, Dickinson's living dead has not been saved from blindness. In some ways, this line points back to the spiritual struggle that Dickinson felt right before her college days. Many of us had our own spiritual struggles during our late teens and well into college. It is clear she wanted to see, but could not. No one can know what Emily Dickinson's final spiritual views were in her life or if she had made that earlier commitment of faith and afterward struggled with a great doubt. If you read the greater body of her poems, you sense a constant struggle with belief in a benevolent, omniscient, and all-powerful God. Nevertheless, with this poem, one sees a heartbreaking poem of spiritual struggle and failure that ends in double blindness. She recognizes a King, but the King of what?

Newton's hymn, stanza by stanza, expands time from past to present to future for the speaker, until we even see the future of not only the speaker but all God's chosen as "we" in the final stanza, with "no less days to sing God's praise / than when we'd first begun." Dickinson plays with time, too, but rather than expanding it, she contracts it into this strange explosive moment of the realization of death. But chillingly, she is not able to move beyond it; the speaker seems trapped not only in room and body but also time.

Dickinson uses a strange word just prior to the last stanza—"interposed." It is not a word we often use, and it means to literally "place something between." Between what? It seems to me that this poem takes place between life and death, if such a place can be imagined. That window (or her eyes) occupies the space in between where the fly lands. I wonder if Dickinson might have been reading Shakespeare's *Julius Caesar* where, during the plotting of the murder of Caesar, whom the people wish to choose as king, Brutus says to the conspirators: "What watchful cares do interpose themselves / betwixt your eyes and night?" Interesting, no? The rebels' "watchful cares" were ironic. Anything but caring, they were murderous and focused on Caesar's death. Or more likely, I believe, Dickinson references another famous hymn she would have recognized, "Come Thou Fount of Every Blessing" which contains the lines: "He to rescue me from danger / Interposed His precious blood." In Dickinson's poem, the speaker is past mortal danger. She has already died. And no salvific blood interposes here—only a fly, who perversely will prey upon or lay eggs in the corpse's pooling blood.

Considering Dickinson's emphasis on the eyes here, one might also remember the passage in Mark 8 when Jesus healed the blind man. The man needed a second healing because he saw "men like trees, walking." He could see, but he couldn't make sense of what he was seeing. After all, what does a man or a tree look like to someone who has been blind all his life? He needed a doubly amazing grace to make him completely well so that he could, in the words of Dickinson, "see to see."

By the end of the poem, we might consider an earlier stanza, remembering that the King does show up for this solemn occasion of death. Anybody might recognize this King as Jesus, the God of extreme forgiveness, who says, "Father forgive them for they know not what they do" while the phrase "King of the Jews" is hanging over his own hanging, whose mercy endures forever. Another thing to remember is that the poem's emphasis is on hearing. We begin and end with that fly buzz. It's not a bee; only a fly. We might recall the words from St. Paul's conclusion of the matter in I Corinthians 15:55: "O Death where is thy sting?" Finally, there is no doubt that we hear a hymn in the form, specifically "Amazing Grace," being played behind (or over) this buzz. And one might find some hope, and grace, in that.

Love vs. Time:
W. H. Auden's "As I Walked Out One Evening"

As I Walked Out One Evening

As I walked out one evening,
   Walking down Bristol Street,
The crowds upon the pavement
   Were fields of harvest wheat.

And down by the brimming river
   I heard a lover sing
Under an arch of the railway:
   "Love has no ending.

"I'll love you, dear, I'll love you
   Till China and Africa meet
And the river jumps over the mountain
   And the salmon sing in the street.

"I'll love you till the ocean
   Is folded and hung up to dry
And the seven stars go squawking
   Like geese about the sky.

"The years shall run like rabbits
   For in my arms I hold
The Flower of the Ages,
   And the first love of the world."
But all the clocks in the city

Began to whirr and chime:
"O let not Time deceive you,
   You cannot conquer Time.

"In the burrows of the Nightmare
   Where Justice naked is,
Time watches from the shadow
   And coughs when you would kiss.

"In headaches and in worry
   Vaguely life leaks away,
And Time will have his fancy
   To-morrow or to-day.

"Into many a green valley
   Drifts the appalling snow;
Time breaks the threaded dances
   And the diver's brilliant bow.

"O plunge your hands in water,
   Plunge them in up to the wrist;
Stare, stare in the basin
   And wonder what you've missed.

"The glacier knocks in the cupboard,
   The desert sighs in the bed,
And the crack in the tea-cup opens
   A lane to the land of the dead.

"Where the beggars raffle the banknotes
   And the Giant is enchanting to Jack,
And the Lily-white Boy is a Roarer,
   And Jill goes down on her back.

"O look, look in the mirror,
   O look in your distress;

Life remains a blessing
   Although you cannot bless.

"O stand, stand at the window
   As the tears scald and start;
You shall love your crooked neighbour
   With your crooked heart."

It was late, late in the evening,
   The lovers they were gone;
The clocks had ceased their chiming,
   And the deep river ran on.

When strangers ask me who is my favorite poet, I hesitate to answer.
It is similar to someone asking you what is the best day of your life or what
is your favorite song. There are bound to be a few good ones. If pressed to
name some of my favorite poets, I will invariably mention W.H. Auden.
He had one of the best ears for the music of the English language. He was
forceful in his pronouncements and deeply suspicious of the romantic in
poetry, and I connect with this desire to have an opinion of poetry based
in thought rather than merely emotion, even though I am one who is often
deeply moved by a good poem. William Carlos Williams famously wrote
in his long poem "Asphodel, That Greeny Flower" that "It is difficult / to
get the news from poems / yet men die miserably every day / for lack / of
what is found there." I can imagine Auden responding that this is not true
at all. Most men don't care for poetry and seem to do just fine without it.
Auden wrote in one of his most famous poems, "In Memory of W.B. Yeats,"
that "poetry makes nothing happen."

   If poetry makes nothing happen, it seems poetry criticism makes even
less than nothing happen. Yet here I am writing it, and I often read it. So
poetry is not exactly doing "nothing." However, these days in American
poetry there is very little forceful or even useful poetry criticism, based in
aesthetics, that makes claims about whether the poetry at hand is beautiful
or how it might fail in that labor. To be negatively critical can ruin or at
least limit a career, due to most poetry critics also being poets who don't
want their own work negatively affected if someone else were to retaliate.

The poetry world is very small. Most contemporary criticism, as a result, is mere back-patting and weak generalization of the work without much critical insight into how the poems might be working or *not* working. And since most poetry getting attention these days is overtly political, if one criticizes the aesthetic of a poem about racism or rape, one is likely to be accused of being insensitive if not an outright evil person who must be canceled by the Twitter or Facebook mob.

Poetry can be deeply subjective, but one does think there might be something objective to a good poem. One of my professors in graduate school, the poet Bruce Bond told us: "Maybe, at the end, it *is* all a matter of taste. But you can't begin there. You can never get anywhere with reading poems if you believe that." This is true. While I believe all poets have something of the romantic in them, many of us also insist adamantly that there are good poems and bad poems. And among those good poems, there are few great poems. Among the bad ones are some real stinkers. It is always amusing to me to hear certain poets go on and on about this place to eat Thai food or that place to get the best coffee, but then they want to tear down the idea of taste in poetry. When a recent Best American Poetry (an anthology that appears each year, chronicling the best published poems in a given year) offended the sensibility of a swath of poets, these poets then put together an opposing anthology called *Bettering American Poetry* whose aim it was "to jam dominant systems of taste" and "center voices of resistance." For them, it seems, there is a better, but there should not be a best. I'm not convinced of this at all because I recognize and accept the fact that "best" in poetry is somewhat subjective, unlike best in math or history, which is necessarily more objective. And I very much like it if someone points me to the BEST Thai food in town rather than just the "better." I definitely had the best Thai food of my life in Portland last year. If you are nearby, go to Pok Pok! In the end, we're free to judge our own experiences, but we should be appreciative of the opinions of others. One should be willing to admit these things if only to be honest about how tastes are formed and might be valuable, containing complexities, and not just dreamily hanging around "in the eye of the beholder."

My saying in this last sentence "One should..." is very much like Auden in his criticism. He was full of pronouncements of what constituted meaningful literature and how it should be made: aesthetics and poetics.

You can always find exceptions to the rule of what he demands authoritatively as a critic, but so much of the time you realize that, in general, he is right. And even if he isn't, you realize he is as opinionated about poetry as a good sommelier is about the best wines. He knows more than you; he has tasted the good stuff and can make a profession of it.

Auden was a poet of the Christian faith. He claimed to have had a spiritual awakening in 1933, and he began to regularly take communion in the Anglican church in 1940. The foremost Auden scholar, Edward Mendelson, writes that "Auden's Christianity shaped the tone and content of his poems and was for most of his life the central focus of his art and thought." Auden's book of criticism, *The Dyer's Hand,* is a wonderful book that I would argue gives a strongly Christian perspective on great poetry.

He was an English poet but, in 1939, he moved to the United States and became an American citizen in 1946. As Europe was headed well into the Second World War, Auden grew wary of how political poetry was using certain kinds of rhetoric (the tool of politicians, not poets, he believed) to persuade people to think a certain way. Very much aware of how fascists were using propaganda leading up to World War II, he found this dangerous and much preferred that poetry should be read simply because it was beautiful and could show us the good and the true through that beauty, and through mystery rather than certainty, through plainness rather than romantic blather. He was a traveler, and early in his life wrote books about his journeys to Iceland, China, and Spain (where he attempted to serve as an ambulance driver in the Spanish Civil War). Auden was a very interesting character, to say the least. His biography by Humphrey Carpenter is one of the most entertaining biographies of any poet that I have ever read.

***

"As I Walked Out One Evening" was published first in Auden's book, *Another Time,* in 1940. The setting of the poem is Birmingham, England, where Auden grew up. When he wrote the poem in the 1930s, this city was a growing urban center that had a vibrant cultural scene. In the first few stanzas of the poem Auden develops the setting: Bristol Street, the pavement, the railway, the clocks looming over the city, and the river are combined with a metaphor of wheat fields.

The poem is built of trimeter lines (mostly iambs) in rhyming quatrains. There are a good number of anapests and feminine endings which both add a lilting quality to the verse. The rhyming is ballad-like, the rhymes coming every other line - abcb defe and so on. As a result of the rhymes being so close, it is a very musical poem. The music is emphasized not only in sound but in the meaning throughout. No sooner than the speaker has walked out onto the street, he hears a lover singing. Soon, the clocks chime in their own tune. The lover's song is so imaginative in its romantic silliness that we forgive him for the audacious praise of his beloved.

Auden makes two biblical allusions in the first two stanzas. The first is seeing "the crowds upon the pavement" as "fields of harvest wheat." We recognize that the speaker of the poem has a Christ-like vision in that he sees people in the way that Christ saw them as portrayed in the Gospel of Matthew. After He performs a series of miraculous healings, the crowds clearly have begun to swell. Wild and unconventional poet that he is, Jesus mixes metaphors (first sheep, then a harvest field) as he looks upon them:

> But when He saw the multitudes, He was moved with compassion for them, because they were weary and scattered, like sheep having no shepherd. Then He said to His disciples, "The harvest truly *is* plentiful, but the laborers *are* few. Therefore pray the Lord of the harvest to send out laborers into His harvest." Matthew 9: 36–38

We know these crowds gathered around Jesus are weary, scattered, and many have need of physical healing. Since Auden's narrator uses this very specific allusion, Auden hints from the beginning that he is viewing a vulnerable and broken world in need of fixing. But the brokenness will, at first, be held at bay.

With this tone established, Auden's next stanza begins: "And down by the brimming river / I heard a lover sing," which helps us recall Psalm 137 in which the poet laments being unable to sing a song due to being held captive in Babylon. Of course, the irony of the Psalmist is not lost on us: "How shall we sing the Lord's song in a strange land" is the heart of the song/Psalm. We can make song out of sorrow, not only joy and love. As the German poet Bertolt Brecht famously wrote: "In the dark times / will there also be singing? / Yes, there will also be singing. / About the dark times." Nevertheless, Auden's lover singing of his beloved is only a slave to erotic love, and his passion, his suffering, is a beautiful one full of bizarre claims we can expect of anyone head over heels in love. After all, love is blind. In many ways, that's a good thing. Young love should mostly be blind to the faults or limitations of a beloved.

The lover here, bless him, is a bit clumsy. The first phrase out of his mouth creates an awkward rhyme. "Sing" is supposed to rhyme with "Love has no ending." Technically, for us to hear a rhyme, we hear the sonic repetition from the last stressed vowel to the end of the word. The "-ing" in "ending" is not stressed like the "-ing" in "sing," so the rhyme is slanted and ungainly. Also, the claim that "Love has no ending" is awkward and not actually true. Perhaps God's eternal love has no ending because God *is* love, but every earthly erotic love comes to an end, sooner or later—hopefully "till death do us part," but often times much earlier.

It is typical of Auden's techniques of understatement to locate the lover of this poem beneath the arch of a railway near some industrially-polluted river which, passing through Birmingham, is nowhere close to a pristine natural setting. Auden often forced an overt realism of everyday life onto scenes that otherwise might seem romantic or full of romantic potential. The lover, like anyone who only thinks of his beloved while ignoring his surroundings, doesn't care that the setting isn't ideal. The lover says "I'll love you" three times in the next two stanzas, as if saying so repeatedly can make the love stay. He proceeds by writing some hilarious hyperbole in order to defeat Time with his words: "till China and Africa meet / the river jumps over the mountain / the salmon sing in the street." Notice how the river and the salmon are given powers hyperbolically greater than what we normally witness. Rivers flow down *from* mountains, and salmon might be sung of in the streets by a fishmonger, so we understand the lover's claims here are at the same time wildly imaginative and still somewhat connected to reality. The next bold statements are the opposite of hyperbole and shrink oceans to laundry, a constellation to a flock of geese, and perhaps most strangely of all, years to rabbits. Finally, he gives her a few outlandish terms of endearment: "The Flower of the Ages" and "the first love of the world." Here, she seems to me both Dante's eternal rose and Eve in the garden of

Eden, both feminine entities in paradises outside two ends of the spectrum of mortal time.

If you've ever written a love poem to your beloved or even a letter or a little note for a lunchbox, you know how hard it is to find the right words to capture everything this person means to you. So, you write something unconventional or silly, and this is exactly the right thing to do. Sometimes we say there aren't words, but that's not true. In English, by some estimates, there are around three hundred thousand words. So when someone says "there aren't words" or "I'm speechless" in response to some overwhelming emotion, it really is only the person admitting their inability to put these words together into any kind of suitable response. A poet just has to accept the limitation of the efficacy of words and do what he or she can, but the poet can never truthfully say "there aren't words." The lover in Auden's poem plunges into language from a great height.

However, in the poem, as in any relationship, Time suddenly interrupts him. Figuratively, time takes its toll on erotic love by making into the ordinary and familiar what had begun as exciting and surprising love; the shine wears off and the rose petals fade. As we say, familiarity breeds contempt. But notice here the toll of the clocks is immediately literal. The clocks of the city have reached the top of the hour and they begin to announce their noise. Strangely, these clocks, the physical and man-made representation of metaphysical Time, begin to make not only noise but words. And song. The poem becomes a duel between Eros and Time, and the poet is bearing witness. The news from Time's perspective is not so wonderful. Whereas the lover had a little over three stanzas to declare his perspective, Time has now begun the first of eight and a half stanzas to steamroll him and his romantic dream of love.

We begin in the negative. The clocks say: "O, let not Time deceive you. / You cannot conquer Time." Even though mankind has engineered and built these clocks on the towers of the city, it cannot control the larger aspect of time (especially the way Time ultimately works in concert with Death) beyond the measurements.

Time accuses and derides, and a litany of negativity opens up before us in feeling and in image: "the burrows of the Nightmare," "Justice naked," "Time" as voyeur who interrupts and "coughs when you would kiss," "headaches," "leaks," "fancy" (which is a lesser form of imagination), "appalling snow," broken dancing, the failure to wash one's self fully clean, "wondering what you've missed"… all these are something the lover has forgotten or at least ignored in his blind bliss.

I have two favorite passages from Auden's work. One is the stanza from his poem "A Summer Night" which goes:

> That later we, though parted then,
> May still recall these evenings when
>   Fear gave his watch no look;
> The lion griefs loped from the shade
> And on our knees their muzzles laid,
>   And Death put down his book.

Here, Auden experiences a moment with his friends that he identifies as timeless and gorgeously peaceful. This poem comes out of a real-life experience at the Downs School where Auden was teaching. He called this his "vision of Agape."

The other passage I love by Auden is here in "As I Walked Out One Evening." The eleventh stanza evokes the opposite sentiment of the one just above (which says that we can have a moment in Time where troubles seem to be lifted away miraculously in a state of Grace). The perspective of the poem has been brought indoors where Time begins to interrogate the domestic life, where lovers are known to make their nest. Even though these four lines are terrifying, they are equally gorgeous. A beautiful anxiety, if that is possible:

> The glacier knocks in the cupboard,
>   The desert sighs in the bed,
> And the crack in the tea-cup opens
>   A lane to the land of the dead.

Inside something as small and homey as a cupboard where we store provisions for daily life, there is an overwhelming glacier. We know what glaciers can do; little by little, through eons, they are able to raze mountains.

Not only is there a glacier in this house, but a desert. Where does it take up residence? In the bed. The bed we recognize as a place of rest and of fertility. But if it is overcome by a desert, the bed is stultified. Notice the wonderful chiasmus structuring this stanza. We shrink from the glacier and desert to the diminutive size of the cupboard and bed. But then just as quickly in this domestic atmosphere, we open back out (however, not to be rescued) from "the crack in the tea-cup" to "a lane" which grows monstrous finally into "the land of the dead." The images and the dramatic way Auden presents them are terrifying in scope and meaning.

Time is not done with this lover. He goes on to insult him even further with the Truth of our human predicament. The world is turned perversely upside down as "beggars raffle the banknotes" and "the Giant is enchanting to Jack" and the innocence of Jack and Jill show the boy as a "Roarer" and the girl sexually seduced or even assaulted "on her back." Time thrusts a mirror in the lover's face so he can see his own faults and his distress, rather than being able to look at his beloved. Time does admit that life "remains a blessing," but man in his mortal state doesn't have the capacity to "bless." Only God, ultimately, can bless. This, again, is Auden's anti-Romantic, harsh realism. Time then instructs the lover, rather than to look at himself, to look out a window at his neighbor. "You shall love your crooked neighbor / With your crooked heart."

This is a bizarre turn to the poem that has stymied many a reader, including myself. Time seems throughout these stanzas to have no regard whatsoever for the well-being of our lover, even going so far as to be antagonistic toward him. But in the last two lines of Time's tirade, he gives the lover a possibility. Though erotic love is surely limited and will fail, a different kind of love emerges. And this is the love Jesus refers to as the second commandment, the Golden rule, to love your neighbor as yourself, second only to loving God with all your heart, soul, mind, and strength. Of course, skeptical Time can't help but get a final dig in, pointing out that both the neighbor and the lover are "crooked." As St. Paul tells us, "All have sinned and come short of the glory of God." And yet, though we are fallen, we can "stand," as Time commands twice here at the end of his speech to the lover.

I want to take a second here and come back to my own defense of the lover. Something he sings earlier is actually not silly, but profound. When he says, "I'll love you / Till... / the river jumps over the mountain," he is not completely wrong. Time shows in the picture of a glacier (a frozen river) how a river might jump over a mountain. And when a river of ice does that, we know it is devastating. With an infinite amount of time, the tectonic plates could perhaps move China and Africa to a miraculous meeting. The lover might be ridiculous, but he is not without hope—from a God's-eye perspective of Time, through eons. The lover might have his obvious limitations, but so does Time.

At the end of this poem, the lover gets no reply. Once Time is done with his long and depressing song, the poem ends with one final stanza in the narrator's voice:

It was late, late in the evening
   The lovers they were gone;
The clocks had ceased their chiming,
   And the deep river ran on.

Instead of our lover returning to the poem, notice that the poet writes "lovers" here. They may be gone, but they are now plural. This is promising! And the clocks have finally shut up their bad news, which is also good news. The clocks cease their chiming because they are themselves limited by Time. They speak as if they have ultimate authority, but they don't. Clocks wear out over the years. They are man-made, unlike the river which ends up being a more comprehensive measure of Time, representing nature rather than just human nature (as the clocks do).

The final image of the river may seem a bland one. This is not surprising for Auden who was, as I have mentioned, one of our finest quotidian and anti-Romantic writers. The image may be plain, but it is profound. Rather than having Time controlled by a man-made construction of city clocks, Time now is measured by the river, one of our iconic symbols for Time. The river's presence signals to us a more enduring view of how we measure life's passage, through nature rather than man. Again, this is a God's-eye view where we end. The river, for the philosopher Heraclitus, was always changing and always new, even though it was the same. It has a scope well beyond the boring limitations of city clocks. Time is given a new physical body in this poem, going from clock to river. Perhaps we might think of the resurrected Christ's transformed body, as well, still bearing the marks of time and the world, but having taken on more fluid possibilities and resurrectional power.

And what of the lovers? One might imagine the lovers are in bed, ignoring the clocks, ignoring the river, embracing each other, doing what lovers do, in time.

***

I first read Auden seriously when I was in graduate school. I took an independent study under the direction of William Logan in which I read all of Auden's *Selected Poems* and some of the criticism of, and also by, Auden, especially *The Dyer's Hand*. At the time, I was writing awful love poems. At the end of the fall semester and approaching my final term, my thesis advisor, Professor Logan, had not accepted many of my poems toward my thesis. Logan was trying to push me away from the love poem and more toward dispassionate or even poems of historical interest. But love poems were a huge part of what I loved in poetry.

Professor Logan and I argued and seemed to be at an impasse. The argument wasn't about whether my poems were any good. I realized I was writing poorly. The argument for me was: How could I write a *good* love poem…even the *best* love poem? Half the tradition of poetry passed down to us is love poetry, so what could I do, I asked, to be part of this tradition? Which were the contemporary love poets I could emulate? I remember Logan sighing, as he probably thought it best I give up this emotionally fraught silliness as it was clearly blocking me from an otherwise objectively good verse, but then he made a concession and wrote me a list of poets/poems to consider. Heaney had some good love poems. Yeats, but stay away from the early Yeats, he said. He mentioned Marilyn Hacker, Richard Wilbur, Theodore Roethke, and a few others. It was a start. I now had a way of being more objective with my overwhelming passion if I could discover how other good poets found forms for their feelings. Strangely, within just a few months I had written a thesis whose poems would only a few months later become a finalist for the Yale Series of Younger Poets, one of the most prestigious prizes for a young poet in the U.S. I'm sure my classmates were shocked (I certainly was); they had been reading my inadequate and romantic poems for a couple years. I had a long way to go, but I felt that I finally had made a breakthrough. I wasn't silly enough to *only* write love poems, and I began branching out. But I still, to this day, am attempting the love poem and looking for other poets who aren't afraid of love, trying to see how they get it done, finding the form and the techniques.

Yet, today there aren't many poets writing love poems. Somehow, I feel that the contemporary poetry classroom has beaten it out of us. Like Auden's lover in "As I Walked Out One Evening," love poets are made to seem silly. It is true we easily fall into cliché, and the stunning beauty of the beloved of our poems blinds us to the words we need to write surprising poetry where language is firing on all cylinders. The more skeptical poets of Time's perspective turn away from the love poem and seem to be able to write more profoundly of politics, or Freudian struggles with family, or even nature. Or they just write about poetry itself, spinning their wheels, sometimes in their own beautiful way. Or maybe this aversion to the love poem is a result of having so many great love poems in the tradition, like "As I Walked Out One Evening," so that we would rather take on some less challenging theme. But we know that many of the greatest poems of all Time have been love poems, and the river of them will continue to run, even so far as jumping over a mountain. As Auden wrote, "Love has no ending."

Sheep and Shepherd, Poet and King:
"Psalm 23"

Psalm 23

A Psalm of David

The Lord is my shepherd;
I shall not want.
He makes me to lie down in green pastures;
He leads me beside the still waters.
He restores my soul;
He leads me in the paths of righteousness
For his name's sake.

Yea, though I walk through the valley of the shadow of death,
I will fear no evil;
For you are with me;
Your rod and Your staff, they comfort me.

You prepare a table before me in the presence of my enemies;
You anoint my head with oil;
My cup runs over.
Surely goodness and mercy shall follow me
All the days of my life;
And I will dwell in the house of the Lord
Forever.

When I first began to conceive of these essays as a book, it was initially titled *Poems for Pastors*. I first chose this title (but changed it due to drastically limiting my audience) because I felt that if I could pinpoint my ideal reader, this person would be a pastor, or someone who is a guardian of the word, an expert in exegesis, and someone who understands more than your average person how eternal, powerful, and even incarnate the word, or *logos*, can be. But more than guardians of the word, pastors (consider the root of the word, *pastor*) are guardians of their flocks, helping to guide them toward health, safety, and the way of life.

I want to examine more deeply one of the most famous religious poems in the history of poetry, Psalm 23. In many ways, as I begin, I feel completely baffled as to what I might say. Perhaps it goes without saying that there is a clear difference between a secular poem such as the others in this book and this God-inspired one. Yet I want to pay attention to the poem in the way I pay attention to the contemporary poems in this book, which is to say that I want to read it closely by looking for patterns, understanding its organization, and analyzing its imagery. At the same time, I don't speak or even read Hebrew, so I am dependent upon the translation and the available commentaries to get an idea of what is going on with the poem and how it works. I won't go into specifics as to how one might translate from Hebrew to English, as that is probably the subject of an entire book or series of books. One recent book, *The Grammar of God: A Journey into the Words and Worlds of the Bible*, by Aviya Kushner, takes a wonderfully interesting and personal look at the difficulty and beauty of translation through memoir and a good amount of linguistic study.

Every good translator knows that a perfect translation is impossible. Even the word *translation* is not enough; writers trying to go from one language to the other use the terms *transliteration, version, imitation,* and *mimesis* to get at different meanings for even the word *translation.* The movement from one language to another almost always involves difference (unless one is saying "No!" in English and in Spanish). When translating poetry, especially, one must also reckon with the music of the language; but since different languages have different qualities that make rhythm and sonic repetitions possible, there is no easy solution. Some languages lack things others might have in abundance, such as verbal inconsistencies like gendered nouns or genitive cases. Sometimes you might be able to imitate a sonic repetition, but you have to change the order of the syntax dramatically. Sometimes you can use exactly the same spelling of a word, but the pronunciation is wildly different in the other language. In Spanish there is one word for "citrus blossom" and one for "wheat ear." You can see in my last sentence that in English we have two words for each of these things. There is also the allusive, cultural, or experiential quality of a language that might not carry over in the other. When we say the words "stars and stripes" in an American poem, it means something completely different for a poet in another country.

The other day I posed a question to my Facebook friends, many of whom are creative writers and poets: What is your favorite Psalm and why? The responses were widely varied: Psalms 1, 4, 12, 18, 19, 22, 23, 51, 61, 63, 67, 70, 84, 91, 119, 121 130, 139, and 150. The "why" aspect of the question was answered in many different ways including: for the sake of comfort, music, childhood memory, and even structural aesthetics. But mostly for comfort. It seems to me that we turn to Psalms when we are in trouble and have no other recourse in some difficult or seemingly unbearable situation. It is no wonder to anyone why Psalm 23 is recited at funerals. The valley of the shadow of death becomes bearable, manageable, or even overcome, finally, through these beautiful words.

I did have one Facebook friend, presumably an atheist, who brought up Psalm 137, which I had been reading just a few days prior. He wanted to point out the horrible aspect of the last few verses where the "little ones" of Babylon are dashed against the rock in some kind of violent revenge. Of course, this "eye for an eye" treatment of justice is hard to contemplate and, I would argue, not even recommended by the text. I would argue that the desire for retributive justice is surely felt and sometimes enacted, but God calls us repeatedly to love our neighbor as ourselves. The Facebook friend who posted this sarcastic comment erased it, presumably after seeing how many others responded so favorably to my original question about which Psalms were favorites.

However, in the world of contemporary poetry, there are few Christians, few who would claim to be born again (as Jesus said you must be), or believers even in the personal and loving Hebrew God of The Bible. And I would say that many of the poets I know who might consider themselves to go by that name of Christian are more full of doubt than your average church-goer. In the world of contemporary poetry, I often feel spiritually lonely. It seems to me that very few are able to say, as Paul said: "For I am not ashamed of the gospel of Christ, for it is the power of salvation to everyone who believes." Poets might share my zeal for the word, but not for the Word. I admit that for many years I have been among those who occasionally find themselves somewhat ashamed of walking the path that early believers lived and died for, what is called The Way.

But more and more as I grow older and, hopefully, wiser, I understand to be true what Peter asked: "Lord, to whom shall we go? You have the words of eternal life." Notice he says not only the eternal life, but the *words* of it. If I am a word guy, that's hard to beat. And I only need look at many of our greatest poets such as Dante, Donne, Milton, Herbert, Eliot, Auden, and so on to find a strong brotherhood of the faith. But being a Christian doesn't mean you'll be a good poet; and being an atheist doesn't mean you'll be a bad one. And vice versa. We all know this is the same for surgeons and mechanics. There's the job to do, and one's theology might have little or nothing to do with it. For poets, there's a lot more than capitalization when it comes to the difference of Word and word. There is the practical knowledge of how language works mechanically via parts of speech, grammar, syntax, rhetoric, etc.

***

Psalm 23 was composed by King David, just about any Bible will tell you. We find it just past halfway into the first grouping of 41 Psalms (Traditionally, there are five groupings in total, which some scholars suggest imitate the organization of the first five books of the Bible). The Psalms are poems, mostly using what is called parallelism to build their structural forms. A line is put down and another line extends the thought in parallel, which is repeated throughout the Psalm. The Proverbs are also structured this way. Just as there are many kinds of secular poems, there are also many kinds of spiritual poems or Psalms of the Bible: praise, lament, thanksgiving, etc. having to do with trust, kingship, wisdom, etc. and combinations of all these.

Many were written by King David, and in times past the Psalms were largely understood to mirror strictly some aspect of the biography of the poet. However, we must realize that all songs do not exactly mirror some biographical aspect of a life. Song lyrics can particularize and generalize and take from the stories of others or even prophesy things that haven't happened yet. We see in the Psalm preceding the 23rd, that David's words of suffering end up mirroring exactly what Christ suffers on the cross in so many ways. It is astonishing when Jesus cries out David's song, "My God, My God, why have You forsaken me" (a song wildly, painfully, but not senselessly crying out for comfort) among his last breaths, though His life was clearly different than King David's. Descended from that earlier king, Jesus was an entirely different kind of King who underwent a far greater suffering, physically and spiritually.

We can learn a great deal of wisdom from this. So many people cry out curses and denials when in mortal danger and agonizing pain; these moments draw us near to God even in our language. We might joke about how after a breakup we search for the saddest songs to comfort us, but clearly there is something to this kind of pathos we can find in the well-sung suffering of others. The blues go back a long, long way. Very few poems are poems of praise. The vast majority are poems of complaint.

Also, I'm not advocating curses, as the Bible instructs us to bless and curse not, and surely Jesus spoke many blessings upon those around Him while bleeding out and suffocating to death. In an interview with the poet/singer Bono, the famous Biblical translator Eugene Peterson argues wonderfully about learning "to cuss without cussing." David himself even allows for cursing in II Samuel 16 when a man named Shemei, a descendent of Saul, comes out cursing the king at a desperate time, when David's own son, Absalom is seeking to kill him. David understands that God can turn it around as he turned around Joseph's plight in Egypt. He says, "It may be that the Lord will look on my affliction and that the Lord will repay me with good for his cursing this day."

What do we know of David, this greatest of spiritual songwriters? We know that he goes from being a shepherd to being a king. Is it any wonder that at the birth of Christ, these two groups are famously warned of his birth and to make haste to come and worship. The shepherds come from the fields, and the kings (or wise men) come from their distant lands. The shepherds presumably come with little or nothing (maybe some good cheese), and the kings come with fine gifts. But isn't that the way? God only asks we bring what we have. In relation to wealth, this is little. Both probably came with songs. If anyone had access to music and the time for it, it was kings. As a king, you can always hire the best musicians to come into your courts and entertain you with good music and stories. This kind of pastime for the wealthy and powerful goes all the way back to Homer's *The Odyssey*. Phemius and Demodocus are both poets/singers who bring people to tears with their words. And shepherds, of course, are famous for being out in the fields with little or nothing to do but move the sheep from pasture to pasture to find new grass, to shear them and milk them and, in between, to sing songs to mostly keep themselves from going mad.

So it is natural that David had, at both ends of the spectrum as king and singer, the skillset for being a good poet. We know that he had plenty to write about—plenty of witnessing the glory of God in so many ways, from the beauty of nature out in the fields, great stories (killing a bear and a lion! and later a giant!), warfare, love, lust, friendship, and personal suffering, some of which he brought on himself, including running for his life on several occasions and the loss of a son. A word of advice, though—Don't ever say to a poet of his suffering, "Well, at least you'll get a poem out of it." Don't say that. No writer wants to hear that.

***

The Psalm of David that begins "The Lord is my shepherd" is clearly a personal one. David, the runt of the litter of his own family, was a shepherd. We remember the story of Samuel coming to anoint the king of Israel. He knew it was one of Jesse's eight sons, and finally after not finding him among all his brothers, they sent for the lad out in the field. When he saw the boy, Samuel immediately knew whom he would anoint. The word *anointed* means "set apart." I suppose that since David was sent back out to take care of the sheep for a while longer, his brothers must have thought "set apart" had a different connotation than savior. The timeline isn't exactly clear, but it seems that even after Saul had brought on David to be his personal singer and armor bearer, David was still partly on sheep duty. Before he fights Goliath, he is being sent back and forth to carry bread and cheese to the troops, to the so-called real men. Ah, the life of poets. And then, even after slaying Goliath, Saul has to ask David his name. Ah, poetry.

Once when I was on a Fulbright Fellowship to the University of Barcelona, my family and I traveled to the Basque country. In a small town in Southern France on market day, my family and I came across a woman selling cheese. "Taste this," she said. It was a cheese made, she told us, by a young shepherd "over in that direction," and she pointed to a distant hill beyond the town. It was amazing, and we savored it. "But this cheese," she said while pointing to another wheel, "this cheese was made by a much older shepherd from over in that direction." We tasted it, and it was even better than the first. We guessed that the young shepherd had some things to learn. Before this, I had never thought of shepherds as the ones who make the cheese. I suppose I just thought of them as the ones leading the sheep around to new pastures and still waters and a yearly shearing, but there is clearly a lot more work going on behind the scenes, even the making of the cheese. And then there is the real-life stuff beyond shepherding like having a family, perhaps, or slaying giants and running a kingdom.

David's prior experience with tending the sheep allows us to see this first verse of the poem as more than mere poetic metaphor. David knows what a shepherd is. Look at how he lifts up the Lord by lowering himself to the level of the sheep. We'll see, many hundreds of years later, in the person of Jesus this same radical humility. He is known as the Lamb of God.

You can find out from anybody who owns a farm that sheep are, by nature, pretty stupid and helpless. They need a shepherd for protection from predators, and they also need to be led to pastures and to still waters. And these waters are not only for drinking. To literally see oneself in ancient times, before mirrors, "still waters" might do the trick. Metaphorically, this looking at one's image is not just to make sure that your hair looks good or you don't have cilantro stuck in your teeth. We can see that a look at the self can be metaphorical. As the scriptures teach, repentance is the first step toward salvation: to see oneself in one's true state and to turn from that. And this cold look at the self is what David is doing by comparing himself to this animal. Some have called this state in need of repentance: "total depravity." Sheep might be seen as "wanting," yet they have someone who cares for them so they "shall not want," and who takes them to beautiful natural settings. God not only will feed us and meet our needs, but he must lead us through treacherous places, perhaps through valleys and among wolves and enemies, through the dangers of our own sin and limitations, to get to other higher ground where we can live more fully.

Launching out beyond the metaphor, we see that the Lord "restores my soul." We are not just sheep; we have souls and need righteousness. And the righteousness is no self-righteousness; it is for His name's sake. All glory goes back to God in the way that the sheep are only really there for the shepherd's food and clothing. Of course, metaphors have their limits; God doesn't need us or food. He wants our fellowship alone. We are there for His glory and His name's sake. I admit it is hard to wrap my head around that, but I take it by faith. As a father who doesn't expect his own children to ever have to care for me or to pay me back anything, I kind of get it. The relationship of love alone is enough. It is all. And yet, when my children love me in return, our relationship is even more fulfilling.

After the rod and staff add to the greater scope of the metaphor with their associations of guidance and discipline, the metaphor then fades away. The last two verses are purely located in the human world of this life and then the life beyond. Sheep don't sit at a table. And this table is *prepared for us*, not just set up. Though "God helps those who help themselves" may be a wise statement in some respects, it is not to be found in the scriptures. Instead we see that all good things come from God, and He even cares enough to set the table and provide the feast. Not only that, we are anointed with oil (again, remember, this means *set apart*), and we have good drink to go with the food, so much so that God doesn't mind filling it to over-flowing, making a bit of a mess. Maybe a party. "In the presence of my enemies" is odd, but it's true enough. Here in this life, we have folks whose main goal seems to be to bring us down. As believers, we don't get an immediately free ticket to Six Flags Over Heaven where all the rides have no wait time. There are difficulties all around us, most of them brought on by our own mistakes. But here the scripture wants to teach us that we can be safe and sound despite our circumstances.

I once heard a pastor preaching a message on putting on the armor of God. He talked about "the breastplate of righteousness," "the helmet of salvation" and "the sword of the Spirit" at length. Finally, to end his sermon he noted that despite all this armor, what would we do when the enemy sneaks up behind us? It may have been a reach, but he cited this last verse of Psalm 23, and claimed: "goodness and mercy shall follow me all the days of my life." I found some wit and some comfort in that.

The poem, this psalm, ends with the statement: "and I will dwell in the house of the Lord forever." We are no longer in a metaphorical pasture, treated like sheep, and no longer in danger among our enemies. We are safe and sound at home with God.

If we lower ourselves in humility, perhaps we can have the promise of being lifted up to the inheritance of a good house, even as David moved from being out in the fields and the wilds into the finest castle where he would rule as king. And isn't this the American dream—to move out from being dependent on our parents (our first shepherds), to own our own house and raise our family there? Yet, even in that movement from humility to independence, we should see that the world and its provision can never be enough. We die, and have no power to defy our destined end. Nothing earthly ultimately satisfies; though our world, especially our American materialistic culture, can never let us believe that. We are inundated constantly with the lie that this product or that program, toy, or drug will finally bring us satisfaction and healing. We know from the story in I and II Samuel that David, after achieving the most astonishing victories with God on his side, wants only more and more, even his neighbor's wife. Like many of us, he has to learn the hard way about worldly desires.

The Bible does tell us that God calls David "a man after my own heart." Somehow I think that probably has more to do with the humility of his shepherding and poetry than his violent kingly ways later on. God roots for the underdog, even the undersheep. Remember, "Does he not leave the ninety nine and go to the mountains to find the one that is straying?" We understand through the sermon on the mount that humility, meekness, gentleness, kindness, and the poor in spirit are the blessed inheritors of the kingdom.

David's primary literary device in this psalm is metaphor. Metaphors are always limited by their range of associations and can only give us a representation of real life. We are not sheep; we are humans. And beyond being mortal humans, we are souls made for eternity. So, in the bigger picture, if we are to learn anything from this poem, we must understand there is more to life than an earthly house or earthly romance as our goal, but the Lord's house. And "forever," which is the last word here, takes us into a realm we can't quite know. We live within the limitations of time, so we must take it by faith. But we also yearn for understanding. We need poetry for that revelation, to at least get close to a perception of the world beyond, which is always described through metaphor as something very much like this one.

Who Will Say Our Names?:
Charles Martin's "After 9/11"

After 9/11

We lived in an apartment on the ridge
Running along Manhattan's northwest side,
On a street between the Cloisters and the Bridge,

On a hill George Washington once fortified
To keep his fledglings from the juggernaut
Cumbrously rolling toward them. Many died

When those defenses failed, and where they fought
Are now a ball field and a set of swings
In an urban park: old men lost in thought

Advance their pawns against opponents' kings
Or gossip beneath a sycamore's branches
All afternoon until the sunset brings

The teenagers to occupy their benches.
The park makes little of its history,
With only traces of the walls or trenches

Disputed, died by, and surrendered; we
Tread on the outline of a parapet
Pressed into the asphalt unassertively,

And on a wall descending to the street,

Observe a seriously faded plaque
Acknowledging a still unsettled debt.

What strength of memory can summon back
That ghostly army of fifteen year olds
And their grandfathers? The Hessians attack

And the American commander folds;
We could have watched those losers made to file
Past jeering victors to the waiting holds

Of prison ships from our Tudor style
Apartment building's roof.
When, without warning,
Twin towers that rose up a quarter mile

Into a cloudless sky were, early one morning,
Wreathed in the smoke from interrupted flight,
When they and what burst into them were burning

Together, like a secret brought to light,
Like something we'd imagined but not known,
The intersection of such speed, such height —

We went up on our roof and saw first one
And then the other silently unmake
Its outline, horrified, as it slid down,

Leaving a smear of ashes in its wake.
That scene, retold from other points of view,
Would grow familiar, deadening the ache:

How often we saw each jet fly into
Its target, with the same street-level gasp
Of shock and disbelief remaining new.

Little by little we would come to grasp
What had occurred, our incredulity
Finely abraded by the videotape's

Grim repetitions. A nonce community
Began almost at once to improvise
New rituals for curbside healing; we

Saw flowers, candles, shrines materialize
In shuttered storefronts for the benefit
Of those who'd stopped the digging with their cries

And those who hadn't. None came out of it,
None would be found still living there, beneath
The rubble scooped up out of Babel's pit:

From the clueless anonymity of death
Came fragments identified by DNA
Samples taken from bits of bone and teeth,

But that was later. In those early days
When we went outside, we walked among the few
Grieving for someone they would grieve for always,

And walked among the many others who,
Like ourselves, had no loss as profound,
But knew someone who knew someone who knew

One of the men who fell back as he wound
A spiral up the narrow, lethal staircase
Or one of those who tumbled to the ground,

The fall that our imaginations trace
Even today: the ones we most resembled,
Whose images we still cannot erase....

One night we joined our neighbors who'd assembled

For a candlelight procession: in the wind,
Each flame, protected by a cupped hand, trembled

As though to mimic an uncertain mind
Feeling its way to some insufficient word —
What certitude could our searching find?

Those who had come here to be reassured
Would leave with nothing: nothing could be said
To answer, or have answered, the unheard

Cries of the lost. Yet here we had been led
To gather at the entrance to the park
In a mass defined by candles for the dead,

As though they were beyond us in the dark
With those who, after their war had been lost,
Surrendered and were marched off to embark

On the waiting prison ships. Here now at last,
They were restored to us in a sublime
Alignment of the present with the past.

But none appeared to mock this paradigm:
All that has come before us lies below
In layer pressing upon layer....
                                    Time

Is an old man telling us how, long ago,
As a child in Brooklyn he went out to play,
And prodding the summer earth with his bare toe

Discovered a bone unburied in the clay,
A remnant of those bodies that once filled
The hulks that settled into Wallabout Bay;

Time is the monument that he saw built
To turn their deaths into a victory,
Its base filled with their bones dredged out of silt;

Time is the silt grain polished by the sea,
The passageway that leads from one to naught;
Time is what argues with us constantly

Against the need to hold them all in thought,
Time is what places them beyond recall,
Against the need of the falling to be caught,

Against the woman who's begun to fall,
Against the woman who is watching from below;
Time is the photo peeling from the wall,

The busboy, who came here from Mexico
And stepped off from a window ledge, aflame;
Time is the only outcome we will know,

Against the need of those lost to be claimed
(Their last words caught in our mobile phones)
Against the need of the nameless to be named

In our city built on unacknowledged bones.

There are few good poems in *terza rima* in English, and there are perhaps even fewer good poems about the terrorist attacks on the World Trade Center of September 2001. Tens of thousands of poets and citizens tried to find words to deal with the loss and silence that death brings, but the bulk of them failed to write a good poem. It's one thing to write a poem as a kind of therapy for yourself or as a kind of personal message to someone close to you, but it's another to write a good poem that any lover of poetry will appreciate. You can't say we don't try.

I have mentioned this before, but it bears repeating: so many of us will say in the face of death and destruction: there aren't words. Because sometimes silence and listening are best. But a poet can rarely say this. A poet knows that there are hundreds of thousands of words in the English vocabulary, and he must arrange them to build a sufficient memorial to any great moment. It is the poet's job to find the words that fit and declare the truth and the experience of life.

But why did the 9/11 poets mostly fail? Robert Frost said that "Poetry begins in delight and ends in wisdom." Political poetry fails so often because it turns this statement on its head, so that the poet believes that poetry begins with wisdom, but then delight is nowhere to be found. The worst of the 9/11 poems thought they knew who or what was to blame, even if they were blaming themselves. Or the poems were only full of complaint and despair. What nearly all these poems had in common was that they stated the obviously awful pain we suffered without finding the beautiful and original language that could sufficiently honor these dead. Most wrote what everyone else would have written (crashing airplanes, falling buildings, fire, ash, sorrow, grief) and exactly what we expected. Great poems always give us what we never expect. You would think that Charles Martin's "After 9/ll" would be an impossible poem to write. It is impossibly good.

Some might not think of a 118-line poem as a "long poem," but when you see the dearth of poems in English *terza rima* written with an essential and cleanly rhyming iambic pentameter, you tend to think of this kind of poem in different terms. Dante had an easier time mastering the rhyme in the vernacular Italian, for sure. The only other recent poem worth reading in English *terza rima* I can think of is Greg Williamson's "On the International Date Line." Richard Wilbur, who recently passed away, was perhaps our best contemporary master of the iambic pentameter line. He has a poem called "Terza Rima" in the form, but it is only sustained for seven lines. Who doesn't shrink, literally and literarily, in the face of Dante's formal achievement?

The pattern of terza rima creates, formally, a kind of logic that can be associated with how the rhyme works. Lines one and three rhyme, and then line two of that same stanza will rhyme with lines one and three of the next. This creates a movement that some call: "two steps forward, one step back." The sonic movement of the rhyme between lines one and three, forward, is pulled back to the second line, which will then carry us to the next stanza, and so on. It creates a link and unity among the stanzas and a kind of thoughtfulness implicit to the form. The rhyme feels its way forward slowly, it goes back a step, and then it moves forward again. Obviously, that is perfect for Dante's epic poem based upon a journey that he must take in order to avoid eternal damnation. Since he must pass through hell and purgatory on his way to paradise, he must watch (often, quite literally) his steps as if his life depended on it—his eternal life.

Many poets consider Dante to be the greatest poet who ever lived. There is no doubt he is *one* of the greatest. *The Divine Comedy* is a poem of utter mastery—formally, mathematically, philosophically, architecturally, spiritually, linguistically, poetically, lyrically, historically, narratively, scientifically, and many would argue—theologically. It is much easier to rhyme in Italian or any romance language than in English, which is comparatively rhyme poor, and this is one of the basic reasons that Dante's form is not quite workable for most poets writing in America.

***

Imagine a generation of people several hundred years from now who cannot remember the 9/11 terrorist attacks. Impossible? Less than 250 years ago, ten thousand captured American men died unimaginably slow and torturous deaths just off the Manhattan coast in Wallabout Bay where they were imprisoned in the holds of the ships there. When they were sufficiently dead, their bodies were thrown overboard, a few washing up on the shores where they were retrieved and could be buried properly. In his poem, Martin does not try to describe this. Rather, he faces the cold fact of our having forgotten our dead: four times the number of dead from the World Trade Center attacks. Four times! Imagine forgetting this kind of human terror. Imagine not a quickly horrifying death, but a languishing death of agonizing rot in the prison of the filthy hold of a ship. But the truth is, we don't want to imagine that. Wouldn't we want to forget it?

We hear the politicians and the optimistic among us cry, "We will never forget." But we do forget. In many ways, we need to move past remembering the afflictions of life toward forgetfulness so we can live beyond death and trauma. Oblivion is both the salve and the festering wound, the drug that soothes and at the same time destroys. By virtue of this poem's form, like Dante's own greatest of poems, "After 9/11" summons us back through a repetition of rhyme that lends itself to the pace of crisis, to the patient equivalent of two steps forward and one step back, to a question of how we remember or fail to do so, to our dead, to a re-orientation of our lives in order that we might be saved. In a plain vernacular Dante would approve of, Charles Martin writes of the towers "burning":

> Together, like a secret brought to light,
> Like something we'd imagined but not known,
> The intersection of such speed, such height—

These towers then "unmake" (a term Dante famously used—Purgatorio 5.134) their outlines and the scene, by virtue of an almost endless repetition on television. And then, despite our memory, the horror "Would grow familiar; deadening the ache." "Grim repetitions," Martin writes, and this is a result of what Time perpetuates against us. Toward the end of the poem, the anaphoric use of the words "Time" and "Against" portray our annihilation through the repetition of the moments that add up to that monster, Time, reminding us of Auden's own famous refrain: "Time will say nothing but I told you so."

However, Martin's "After 9/11" is certainly more influenced by Auden's other poem obsessing over Time's curse upon us: "As I Walked Out One Evening." In that poem, the clocks of the city make a long rant against the ridiculous poet who sings in the street of his everlasting love. The clocks use a similar anaphoric repetition, saying, "you cannot conquer Time" and "Time watches from the shadow / and coughs when you would kiss" and "Time will have his fancy / tomorrow or today" and "Time breaks the threaded dances."

You can see in the concluding stanzas that "Time…Against…us" is Martin's final theme. The ticking of the clock is hypnotic, and we must ultimately sleep. Any poem may suffer its own repetition of rhyme, of anaphora, of historical duplications, because the danger of repetition is tedium. But repetitions (especially rhyme) with carefully constructed variations are powerful mnemonic devices as well. And in the hands of Martin, conjuring the power of Auden's anti-romantic Truth, we are faced with our failure of forgetfulness leading to death.

Time ultimately defeats our memories and histories and joys and pains, but we have the weapon of memorable language, especially poetry, to raise up in our defense. Poetry, while seemingly weak and certainly less popular than any other form of writing, is our greatest ally.

Ironically, Martin's poem ends almost hopelessly: "Against the need of the nameless to be named / In our city built on unacknowledged bones." Martin is right: for who remembers the dead of Wallabout Bay? Who has ever heard of the ones who died at the very birth of our country fiercely seeking its independence, liberty, and individual human freedoms we mostly take for granted? Not one in ten thousand you might ask on the street would have any idea. But the poem itself, this poem, signifies that while we are already in the midst of forgetting the dead of 9/11 (we hate to believe this awful truth), perhaps only poetry can restore the forgotten dead, giving these "unacknowledged bones" the power to rise up and walk. These "bones" are the final word. Yet, see what he has done. He has resurrected them for us. You and I, who never knew who they were, now know because of poetry.

If I am hopeful, I am reminded of John Donne's "Death, thou shalt die." But if I let Time have her say, I am taken back to the beginning of this poem where I realize the first words of the poem are "We lived...." In the primary sense of the poem, this is only a reference to the time the speaker once lived in New York City. But in another sense, one surely sees this phrase as the past tense of *to live*. Any good reader knows that from the very beginning death is knocking on our door, and Time is the measure of the awful silence between those knocks. We are in need of a salvation beyond the juggernaut of Time. *Juggernaut*, a battleship, etymologically means "Lord of the things that move" or in other words, "Lord of the living." But this lord, Time, is a master who crushes the living under his steady wheels. What happens to each us when the motion of our gears and wheels finally stops? Who will remember us and say our names?

***

I recently made a trip to the National September 11 Memorial and Museum and the site surrounding it, where 2,753 people died that fateful morning of September 11, 2001. The memorial is beautiful and brought tears to my eyes. A lot of thought and money has gone into these grounds. Remarkably, the price tag of the project came to around half a billion dollars ($329 million which came out of federal HUD funds). To me, the most striking aspects of the site are the two shiny black granite coated reflecting pools that now cover the former footprint of the two destroyed buildings. The names of those who died there in the terror attack are carved into the outer edges. In each, water spills down from the sides into a large pool and then disappears into yet another square at the center of this pool into what I can only describe as an abyss. When looking at it, I felt a great sense of sadness, despair, and dread. *This is hell*, I thought. Between these two pools rises a giant white rib cage/winged structure called The Oculus, designed by Santiago Calatrava, which is both a retail center and a subway transportation hub whose cost has exploded to a whopping $4 billion price tag, double what was initially proposed. The visual effect of these white wings rising between the two black abysses is perhaps as breathtaking as the price tag. Towering far above this is the new One World Trade Center, 1776 feet high, the tallest building in the Western Hemisphere. Tragedy may strike but life, transportation, and commerce go on.

The memorial in Fort Greene Park for the war dead who died in Wallabout Bay aboard those horrible prison ships is, by contrast, ordinary and somewhat ignorable. Dedicated in 1908 with President-elect William Taft delivering the address, it is a simple 149 foot Doric column of granite with a giant bronze urn on top and a simple inscription at its base: 1776 THE PRISON SHIP MARTYRS MONUMENT 1908. It stands atop a crypt which contains a small portion of the bones of the war dead. One morning I went for a run in Brooklyn which included a brief jog through Fort Greene Park. Passing by the monument, I saw a dozen or so young people doing pilates exercises in unison on the level slab in front of the memorial.

Race and Civilization:
Countee Cullen's "Heritage"

Heritage

(for Harold Jackman)

What is Africa to me:
Copper sun or scarlet sea,
Jungle star or jungle track,
Strong bronzed men, or regal black
Women from whose loins I sprang
When the birds of Eden sang?
One three centuries removed
From the scenes his fathers loved,
Spicy grove, cinnamon tree,
What is Africa to me?

So I lie, who all day long
Want no sound except the song
Sung by wild barbaric birds
Goading massive jungle herds,
Juggernauts of flesh that pass
Trampling tall defiant grass
Where young forest lovers lie,
Plighting troth beneath the sky.
So I lie, who always hear,
Though I cram against my ear
Both my thumbs, and keep them there,
Great drums throbbing through the air.

So I lie, whose fount of pride,
Dear distress, and joy allied,
Is my somber flesh and skin,
With the dark blood dammed within
Like great pulsing tides of wine
That, I fear, must burst the fine
Channels of the chafing net
Where they surge and foam and fret.

Africa? A book one thumbs
Listlessly, till slumber comes.
Unremembered are her bats
Circling through the night, her cats
Crouching in the river reeds,
Stalking gentle flesh that feeds
By the river brink; no more
Does the bugle-throated roar
Cry that monarch claws have leapt
From the scabbards where they slept.
Silver snakes that once a year
Doff the lovely coats you wear,
Seek no covert in your fear
Lest a mortal eye should see;
What's your nakedness to me?
Here no leprous flowers rear
Fierce corollas in the air;
Here no bodies sleek and wet,
Dripping mingled rain and sweat,
Tread the savage measures of
Jungle boys and girls in love.
What is last year's snow to me,
Last year's anything? The tree
Budding yearly must forget
How its past arose or set—
Bough and blossom, flower, fruit,
Even what shy bird with mute

Wonder at her travail there,
Meekly labored in its hair.
One three centuries removed
From the scenes his fathers loved,
Spicy grove, cinnamon tree,
What is Africa to me?

So I lie, who find no peace
Night or day, no slight release
From the unremittent beat
Made by cruel padded feet
Walking through my body's street.
Up and down they go, and back,
Treading out a jungle track.
So I lie, who never quite
Safely sleep from rain at night—
I can never rest at all
When the rain begins to fall;
Like a soul gone mad with pain
I must match its weird refrain;
Ever must I twist and squirm,
Writhing like a baited worm,
While its primal measures drip
Through my body, crying, "Strip!
Doff this new exuberance.
Come and dance the Lover's Dance!"
In an old remembered way
Rain works on me night and day.

Quaint, outlandish heathen gods
Black men fashion out of rods,
Clay, and brittle bits of stone,
In a likeness like their own,
My conversion came high-priced;
I belong to Jesus Christ,

Preacher of Humility;
Heathen gods are naught to me.

Father, Son, and Holy Ghost,
So I make an idle boast;
Jesus of the twice-turned cheek,
Lamb of God, although I speak
With my mouth thus, in my heart
Do I play a double part.
Ever at Thy glowing altar
Must my heart grow sick and falter,
Wishing He I served were black,
Thinking then it would not lack
Precedent of pain to guide it,
Let who would or might deride it;
Surely then this flesh would know
Yours had borne a kindred woe.
Lord, I fashion dark gods, too,
Daring even to give You
Dark despairing features where,
Crowned with dark rebellious hair,
Patience wavers just so much as
Mortal grief compels, while touches
Quick and hot, of anger, rise
To smitten cheek and weary eyes.
Lord, forgive me if my need
Sometimes shapes a human creed.
All day long and all night through,
One thing only must I do:
Quench my pride and cool my blood,
Lest I perish in the flood,
Lest a hidden ember set
Timber that I thought was wet
Burning like the dryest flax,
Melting like the merest wax,

Lest the grave restore its dead.
Not yet has my heart or head
In the least way realized
They and I are civilized.

Even as I begin this essay, in many ways, I hesitate to write it. These paragraphs will ultimately involve the subject matter of race, and there is probably no more divisive thing in this contemporary world of 2020 than the color of one's skin. As a nation, it seems we are constantly polarized when it comes to issues involving race and the politics surrounding it. As a white man, I am in a position of privilege and, in many ways, cannot experientially speak to the sufferings of others who have been discriminated against daily on the basis of their skin color. But I bear witness to discrimination and racist acts and language quite often, despite the fact that we all have more in common than we differ.

Race should not be the definitive explanation of any given person's experience or life, our joy or our suffering. Nor should sexuality, class, gender, etc. sufficiently tell the story of who we are. However, for some who feel defined by the people around them or who define themselves according to the color of their skin, these human particularities and characteristics can be overwhelming. Racial discrimination continues to erode our human relationships, and even though the civil rights movement made great strides in changing the laws of our nation, racial tensions seem to be at an all-time high.

Recently, the Black Lives Matter movement has drawn attention to the brutal treatment of black men by police officers and other authority figures. The recent award-winning documentary film *13th* highlights the mass incarceration of black men and how this disproportionate number has been turned into a modern-day industry comparable to slavery in early America. We hear daily of racial threats in public toward darker-skinned people, especially Muslims, due to our various conflicts throughout the Middle East and the 9/11 attacks on the Pentagon and the World Trade Center.

Racial bigotry goes in all directions. Recently, the horrifying torture of a white special-needs child by his African-American classmates made the news. On my Twitter and Facebook feeds, I see a barrage of posts giving advice to "white people," as if that moniker is helpful. I have to tread lightly here. Even addressing the issue, some may think I have gone too far. I have seen numerous calls for "white people" to "just shut up" since we've "had our turn" to speak. A white poet recently became infamous when he was discovered publishing his poems under an Asian-sounding name (so he could "have an edge," he claimed), while an up-and-coming black poet recently wrote an inflammatory poem called "Dear White America." There seems no end to our lashing out, judging and hurting each other on the basis of the colors of our skin rather than the content of our character. Most recently, minority students at Evergreen College, one of the most liberal colleges in America, called for a day without white people on campus. A white professor who refused to abide by this call was warned by the campus police that he was taking his life into his own hands. And in Charlottesville, at the University of Virginia, we recently watched young white men marching together carrying torches, some chanting "blood and soil," an old Nazi saying, in their protest against the removal of Confederate statues. Shortly thereafter at a peaceful counter-protest against these men, a man drove a car into a crowd, killing one of the protestors. As I write this, the entire nation is in turmoil over the killing of George Floyd, a police officer having kneeled upon his neck for nearly nine minutes in broad daylight while his fellow officers stood by. While most of us, day to day, may think we are relatively unaffected by violence and racism, we can't deny that our various heritages and our genetic pasts will continue to intrude on a peaceful present and future.

***

I want to write about Countee Cullen's poem, "Heritage," because it is an extraordinary poem that troubles the waters of race and nationality in a beautiful way, and it directly names Jesus Christ in the volta, or turning point, of this poem. It fits the theme of this book treating poems of deep spiritual meaning. In the same way that I, as a poet and professor, must tread lightly concerning racial issues, so must pastors and Christians in the church (whose call is one of humility) consider their precarious positions of privilege or poverty. It is easy to assume things about other people groups, and it is difficult and sometimes nearly impossible to love one's neighbor, no matter what color or class or religion. But Christians are commanded to do it.

Racial and tribal differences in the Bible are nothing new. When God set apart his chosen people through Abraham according to a genetic/familial grouping, he certainly created a problem for us. Or was the "issue" already there, and by God giving a promise to Abraham's seed, did he merely expose the sin already deep within our hearts? Throughout the Bible, we see a differentiation of morals among nations based on genetics and cultures, but we also see a commandment for us to love our neighbors, no matter their backgrounds. The three most obvious references that I see in the books of the New Testament are the story of the good Samaritan, Jesus's own mixed lineage, and Paul saying that if you are in Christ, you are Abraham's seed. Thus the promise of inclusion in the family of God extends to all who love Him and believe in Him. There are an extraordinary number of stories concerning inclusivity as a goal; perhaps as many or more as there are of exclusivity.

If I watch the news for very long or scroll through social media platforms at all, I can feel quite helpless, as though there will never be unity among the races. Is there any way for our country's foundation, very much built on the backs of black slaves, to somehow be repaired? It can if it involves both repentance and forgiveness. One of the most beautiful church services I have ever attended was in New York City, where I attended the Brooklyn Tabernacle one Sunday morning. I don't think I've ever witnessed such unity among diversity, all with one goal of worshipping the living God.

***

Countee Cullen was an African-American poet who wrote in the early 20th century, and is classified among those we call the Modern Poets, or the Modernist Movement. He wrote similarly to Eliot, Stevens, Pound, Moore, Stein, William Carlos Williams, Hughes, and Frost, who were changing poetry forever, turning away from easy pastoral imagery and romantic feeling toward wilder, imagistic juxtapositions and harsher ironies. While I would argue that Cullen wasn't the best poet of the Modern period, his poem "Heritage" is one of the most stunning and skillful poems to come out of it.

The poem is actually forward-looking in its technique, in that the speaker of the poem seems very much like the poet himself. We see a little bit of it in the World War I Poets and more so in the poets of the Harlem

Renaissance. In the other Modern poets, we see almost exclusively the speaker presented at a distance from the poet, using some kind of mask for a more objective voice. For instance, T.S. Eliot as "Prufrock" or Ezra Pound as "Mauberley." Cullen's very personal and emotional perspective does not take root till the Confessional poets wrote their poems many years later.

We see immediately that "Heritage" is written in acephalic iambic tetrameter rhyming couplets. Acephalic simply means "headless" indicating that the unaccented syllable that would normally be at the beginning of the line is just not there. Depending on how one scans poems, one might say that the line is catalectic trochaic tetrameter: the last syllable is cut away. Since the bulk of poetry in English tends toward the iambic, I side with the former. Regardless of what we call it, the thing to notice here is that starting each line with a stressed syllable does cause an extraordinary and energetic effect on the standard iambic four-beat line.

William Blake most famously used this line to write his most famous poem, "The Tyger" whose first stanza looks like this:

Tyger Tyger, burning bright
In the forests of the night;
What immortal hand or eye,
Could frame thy fearful symmetry?

W.B. Yeats, whom many consider to be the best lyric poet in the English language, wrote one of his last poems, "Under Ben Bulben" in the same meter. Note the exacting stresses and his use of slant rhyme:

Swear by what the Sages spoke
Round the Mareotic Lake
That the Witch of Atlas knew,
Spoke and set the cocks a-crow.

Cullen's poem appeared in 1925, years before " Under Ben Bulben" was written. While Yeats veers from the form as the poem goes along, allowing a looser rhythm here and there, if you scan "Heritage," you can hear how Cullen's poem is much more strict throughout. After Yeats died in 1939, Auden wrote several poems in this form. One of his most famous poems, "In Memory of W.B. Yeats," uses this same measure in the last section of the poem to great effect: "Earth receive an honoured guest. / William Yeats is laid to rest" is how this section begins. All three are forceful poems of urgency, and I would argue that the formal quality of having a stressed syllable beginning and ending each line adds to the emotional tenor of these poems.

Cullen's poem begins with a line that becomes a refrain, returning twice more in the poem: "What is Africa to me?" He repeats this line with variation by shortening it to "Africa?" and, shifting the question later to North America, "What is last year's snow to me?" This musical and rhetorical repetition keeps us engaged with the thread of questioning the heritage of place/geography throughout. Prior to the first repetition of this line, Cullen paints a vivid and colorful picture, lush with flora and fauna, harkening back to the cradle of civilization. This looking back is anthropological, historical, familial, and religious (Eden). With this bracketing (a kind of chiasmus— we go into the landscape and then back out) by the question, "What is Africa to me?," Cullen draws his reader into his psyche. At first, the question seems genuinely placed within Africa. The speaker is asking, "Do I think about the jungle or the heavens, my male forefathers or female progenitors, flora or fauna, centuries or millennia, personal or communal?" Notice these oppositions that help to intensify the internal conflict of the speaker.

The choice the speaker has posed to himself, he realizes, is a false one. The next line begins, "So I lie." Now, perhaps we have the lazy poet here reclined upon his bed thinking deeply, as poets do. Remember that T.S. Eliot once claimed that being a poet requires a "necessary laziness." Neither Eliot nor Cullen were lazy in their writing, obviously, so we understand that "So I lie" is more than a recumbent position. Cullen's speaker realizes that, by setting up answers to his question in simple binaries, he is lying to himself. The answer to the question is going to be much more complex. For instance, his desire for "wild barbaric birds" and a land where "young forest lovers lie" should be understood as a simplistic and romantic point of view. But note how this "lie" returns at the end of the sentence to reiterate the complexity of the word. Now it is sexual. It seems, having heard himself say the word "lie" in this new context, he can't help but return to it. He begins his next two sentences with "So I lie," complicating the ways in which he is trying to understand where he is from and who he is.

First, he seems to say that he is always trying to deny his African heritage. He tries to dampen the sound of those African drums he always hears. Second, he realizes that he is, by turns, proud and ashamed of his genetic make-up, his skin and his blood, his outer appearance and his interior life. While he is trying to take pride in an ancestry connected to a wilder background, this "chafing net" symbolizes for him the fact that this wildness was captured, enslaved and shipped across great waters to serve, humiliated, in America. Wildness has its limitations insofar that it can be tamed or enslaved.

Next, he simply says, "Africa?" It is a forceful curtailing of the question into one word. He answers by naming it "a book." As if an entire history, geography and multiplicity of cultures could be summed up in a book. The poet realizes he, himself, is trying to sum these things up in a poem. Of course, you can do in a poem what you cannot do in a history book, and that is to deeply engage unfathomable mysteries and feelings through the music of language. By treating one's own history as a text, however, one must "unremember" simple and natural details so as to get at the more heady topics of what we call history. The natural history of bats, ferocious cats, snakes, and flowers might seem unimportant to an anthropological historian. But not so for the poet. Ultimately, living in North America far from his origins, the speaker asks himself what the natural fact of the snow here and now means, rather than some historical weather/climate centuries or millennia ago. These things are fleeting and insignificant details; not archetypal. His racial crisis has become an existential crisis. A few lines later he will see himself vaguely as "a soul gone mad with pain."

Once more the speaker repeats "What is Africa" and "So I lie." His body then becomes a conflicted landscape of "civilized street" and "jungle track." He finally admits that he is tempted toward this "Lover's Dance" where heathen gods are fashioned and presumably worshipped. In the middle of the sentence, a seemingly ungrammatical interruption happens. To me, it's a "Damascus Road experience" akin to being knocked flat off a horse. Cullen writes:

My conversion came high-priced;
I belong to Jesus Christ,
Preacher of Humility;
Heathen gods are naught to me.

Why this shocking turn? Perhaps the speaker realizes that the pagan practice of idol worship, "the heathen gods / black men fashion out of rods," is completely perverse in relation to the proper order of the universe, according to Genesis 1:26 and Romans 1:25. Rather than man being made in God's image, gods are being made in man's image or other images of creation. Immediately, the Christian poet must reverse the order back to the three-personed God's design. At first, this might seem too easy—the poet resorting to a blind faith to escape his conflicted self. But notice how the speaker confesses, despite his conversion experience, his continued conflict.

One of my students pointed out something absolutely extraordinary to me about the line: "My conversion came high-priced." No one usually thinks about the monetary value of human life, but we cannot deny that there was an actual monetary price paid for chattel slaves. They were auctioned. To use the economic term "high-priced" in relation to the speaker's repentance is to realize also the price to be paid for the redemption of a human being. Of course, for the Christian, the price is the death of the Son of God paid for the spiritual freedom of all mankind, any who would sign their name on the back of this check.

Cullen longs for a savior who is "black," like him. Though converted, he cannot help but sin like those pagans long ago who wanted to make God into their image. He admits as much: "Lord, I fashion dark gods, too." This crowning "with dark rebellious hair" is just one more crown of thorns that he would inflict upon a loving Christ who is not interested in preserving racial division. To do so would be to try and crucify Christ a second time, and "the grave restore its dead." The speaker finally confesses that though he is saved (heart), he is still imperfect (head), and the process of salvation must bear itself out in time for him to be "civilized." This is an odd word to end the poem. *Civilized* is a word that comes from Latin, meaning "of or among a community of people." The poet here realizes he is trying too much to be part of a community outside God's perfect relationship. He is dependent upon the opinions of men and their outward differences rather than their similarities: we are all made in God's image. The poem's ending is disturbing. To be civilized is to deny, in some ways, individuality and freedom, and to perhaps become prey to slavery again.

Christians admit with St. Paul that we are slaves to Christ, but this is no doubt a more difficult metaphor for those who not long ago have literally been in chains due to the color of their skin. There can be no doubt that it is much more a reality for the African-American. The poem ends abruptly, leaving the reader not completely satisfied, yet surely this is a most powerful ending. Great poems most often defy easy closure, and this one is no exception. To paint too rosy a picture of one's deep spiritual struggle might be to diminish the realistic quality of the suffering with some kind of Hollywood ending, riding off into the sunset, all racial strife settled. No one who is paying attention to the news one hundred years after Cullen's poem was written can believe that. Has any one of us escaped being "civilized"? Can we say that we are in the world and not of it, as I John 4 defines the Christian? We may try our best, but we fall short. The last sentence of the poem is firmly in the negative. "Not yet.../ In the least way" has the speaker "realized," and so the struggle continues.

***

Not only our skin color defines us, but even more so our place and our language. In Virgil's *Aeneid*, on the road to Carthage, Venus (in disguise) meets Aeneas and asks him three questions: "Where are you from? Who are you? And where are you traveling?" The answers to these three questions might very well define any human being's essence. The middle question is about the present and might be summed up in a name, but this present person I might be is surely predicated upon what I have done in the past and what I will do in the future. And past and future are not only constructs of time, as Venus shows through her question, but constructs of place.

Another powerful poem on the deep conflicts of an individual dealing with a racial divide is Derek Walcott's "A Far Cry from Africa." Walcott died recently, and many considered him one of the best living poets writing in English. I agree with that estimation, and I recommend to any serious reader his epic poem *Omeros*. In a brilliant, shorter lyric poem, "A Far Cry from Africa," Walcott deeply, in his own way, engages the difficulties of being torn between two racial identities:

The gorilla wrestles with the superman.
I who am poisoned with the blood of both,

Where shall I turn, divided to the vein?
I who have cursed
The drunken officer of British rule, how choose
Between this Africa and the English tongue I love?
Betray them both, or give back what they give?
How can I face such slaughter and be cool?
How can I turn from Africa and live?

Walcott wildly and somewhat "inappropriately" puts himself between gorilla and superman, both fictional fantasies of who we are or might be at our worst or best, animals or gods. "How choose / Between this Africa and the English tongue I love?" Walcott cries out. Like Cullen, he is caught up in a struggle much bigger than himself. Walcott realizes the music of the English language is largely rooted in traditional forms, especially rhyme and the iambic line. Is adopting the tongue of the oppressor giving in to slavery, or is it mastering the master? Even the title of the poem engages in a bit of language play, using a term that both mocks and engages the "cry." As Cullen played with the word "lie," here Walcott allows the cry's ambiguity to create more tension in the poem. Language has this possibility of multiplicity, and you can either harness the power of ambiguity or fall prey to it. Even though he asks, "How choose," in several ways Walcott does "choose." He chooses the English tongue he loves. We can see the traditional formal rhyming he is consciously crafting right in front of us. Walcott ends his poem with five unanswered questions, leaving us in a world of deeply-felt conflict, perhaps even more unsettled than Cullen's speaker in "Heritage."

Others differ on this as to their own poetics, choosing whether to work in traditional forms passed down to us from Eurocentric traditions or working in newer forms of their own devising. Some claim that formal choices can be seen as making a statement on race or even gender. However, there is not one rule about how to make a poem other than to avoid cliché and obvious grammatical mistakes. And even clichés and grammatical mistakes can lend meaning to a poem—if mastered (I do not choose this word lightly) and if we know that the poet is purposely exploring some particular usage.

Cullen and Walcott choose traditional forms rooted in the iamb and rhyme for their lyrics. I don't think anyone could argue convincingly that these poems ultimately fail because they are bound by a traditional formality. On the contrary, they succeed because of their mastery of the traditional forms. Both poets present their conflict realistically and powerfully, complicatedly engaging us if we are good readers to experience them deeply no matter what the color of our skin or the place of our birth.

The Blind Shall See:
A. E. Stallings's "Explaining an Affinity for Bats"

Explaining an Affinity for Bats

That they are only glimpsed in silhouette,
And seem something else at first—a swallow—
And move like new tunes, difficult to follow,
Staggering towards an obstacle they yet
Avoid in a last-minute pirouette,
Somehow telling solid things from hollow,
Sounding out how high a space, or shallow,
Revising into deepening violet.

That they sing—not the way the songbird sings
(Whose song is rote, to ornament, finesse)—
But travel by a sort of song that rings
True not in utterance, but harkenings,
Who find their way by calling into darkness
To hear their voice bounce off the shape of things.

The ancient Greeks considered birds, their flight and behavior, omens of one sort or another. An eagle takes a goose out of the sky, and you had better watch out for trouble around the bend. If you saw a snake with a cardinal's tail feathers sticking out of his throat, you might think that it meant something absolutely awful. It's not always bad news—the things we divine that birds are trying to tell us. I'm not kidding when I tell you that once, not long ago, a bird that had been feasting on our mulberry tree flew over me and dropped his purple excrement on my leg, and a week later I had a contract delivered for the book you now hold in your hands.

Not that it had anything to do with the bird, mind you, but one might wonder.

A few years back, I was teaching a two-week intensive poetry class down in the Texas Hill Country where Texas Tech University has a satellite campus. Another faculty member was teaching an ornithology class at the same time. When I wasn't busy with my own class, I was out on walks or tubing down the river and I would notice a lot of birds. This area of Texas is a major flyway and mid-May brings a big migration shift, so you can see a lot of species if you are paying attention.

I got a local checklist from the professor of the ornithology class, and started a competition with his students. I told them that I would find more species of birds than all of them combined. I had some experience, being a novice birder, so I just went to work keeping my eyes upward. "It's also important to keep your ears tuned," the professor told me. He often located birds, he said, by ear rather than by sight, and would confirm only with a visual authentication. I ended up seeing over 100 species in those two weeks, and the class beat me by 5 or 6 birds. But the whole experience opened my eyes and tuned me in to a world above me I hardly knew existed.

Bats, as any elementary school student will tell you, are not birds, but mammals. And yet their flight seems to be just as magical and important to us stuck here on the ground. When I was a kid living in rural Pennsylvania, we lived on a farm a few miles from town. At the end of our driveway, next to our house, there was a telephone pole with a light on it, where on summer nights bugs would swarm. Bats would emerge from their hiding places in our barn and come to feast. I can remember their jagged, strange, otherworldly flight, vividly emerging from the dark and then disappearing back into it.

We often would throw small stones from the driveway in the air, not to hurt the bats, but to watch them mistake these flying objects for insects. Once, one of the bats followed the stone all the way into the ground where it crashed. I remember my brother picked it up with a stick, and we were all horrified at seeing the thing up close. This was no precious bird that we felt sorry for but a monster, or so it seemed. I believe a lot of people think this way about poems in relation to stories. They just have no idea how to imagine this bizarre shape of words.

***

The sonnet is the poem of the magician and the underdog. It is also the poem of the mathematician, the lover, and the rebel. In its first few hundred years, it was used almost exclusively as a form to convey the thoughts and feelings of love. But in the last few hundred years, the sonnet writer seems to want to make it do something new every time, even while maintaining its basic structural form of fourteen lines of rhyming iambic pentameter, though sometimes pushing those formal boundaries. More recently, it has been used as a form able to express and reflect the political, the personal, the elegiac, the natural world, and even Olympic feats. Its fourteen lines are usually broken up into an eight/six form of octave and sestet. One of the primary effects of this form is to have the final six lines outdo the former eight which have set up some kind of initial argument. Hence, the underdog. In Shakespeare's development of the form, the final two lines often seem to outdo the previous twelve.

There are two primary types of sonnets. The first, the Elizabethan or Shakespearean form, has seven different rhymes, which make it easier for the English practitioner (because English is rhyme-poor compared to Italian) to make a poem without straining too much for multiple rhyme words. The second, the Italian or Petrarchan form, uses only five rhymes at most. The first eight lines are made up of only two rhymes that alternate in a brace rhyme scheme: abbaabba, as seen above in Alicia Stallings' poem. If you think this is not difficult to do in English while developing a clear argument in meter and paying attention to lines and the entire sound/syntax/sense of the octave, give it a try some time.

Like baseball, the sonnet is a game of inches (and feet). The numbers of the stanzas, rhymes, feet, and variations in the overall structure are just as important as the numbers of innings, players on a baseball team, the distances between bases, pitcher's mound, and home plate, and the differences between the speed of a fastball and a slider. It is, if not science, a game of mathematics.

Alicia Stallings is one of the few strong contemporary poets who works almost strictly in form, and one of the few able to pitch a perfect game. From Atlanta, perhaps she is the Greg Maddux of poetry. Her approach to poetry is studied, not merely felt. Her training is classical. Her poems, as well as her translations of Lucretius, Sappho, and Virgil early on in her career have garnered many awards, most recognizably a Guggenheim and a MacArthur Genius Award. Her sonnet here seems, at first, to be a poem about the natural world, but like many of Robert Frost's great nature poems, it goes much further than that, signifying deep spiritual truth.

Stallings's poem begins, via the title, with the presumption that she must explain to us why her speaker has an affinity for bats. Many of us have an irrational fear of bats due to the bloody mythology that surrounds them, even though ironically they actually save us from a lot of bloodsucking due to the number of insects they devour. But there is no denying that their nocturnal habits, their diet of insects, and, up close, their razor-toothed, rodent faces and hairy, jagged skin-wings are slightly terrifying. So, Stallings has some convincing to do.

The first line begins *in medias res*, in the middle of things, viewed from our human perspective below. The bat is in flight, we assume, at evening, in the last light. The decline into darkness has begun. Line two portrays a psychological denial of what we see and imagine, "And seem something else at first—a swallow—," or it is at least a somewhat more familiar image of flight since we are creatures of sight. We don't want to see a bat, so we go with something more angelic than demonic —a bird rather than a rodent: a swallow. Line three, perhaps because it is getting darker, relates the sight to a sense of sound: "move like new tunes, difficult to follow." Line four completes the first brace rhyme with "they yet." So we move from "silhouette" to "they yet." "Yet" is a word which creates uncertainty in the movement of the bat and/or our observation of it. This ending on a rhyme word of such uncertainty reminds me of Robert Frost's "Stopping by Woods on a Snowy Evening," where Frost writes: "Whose woods these are I think I know. / His house is in the village, though." In conversational speech, someone would say something more like: "I think I know whose woods these are, but his house is in the village." A poet, however, wants to do more work with words, to make them mean more, to emphasize them, especially their sound, so Frost allows "though," via rhyme with the previous "know," to resonate aloud and create a feeling of uncertainty. Stallings does the same here with "yet." The rhyme makes us pay more attention to that word.

The second four lines (a quatrain, if you consider the way the brace rhymes cordon off those lines) continue the observation, developing our sense of a binary world: light/dark, sight/sound, bird/mammal, solid/hollow, height/depth. All of these binaries seem to move toward darker, more limited, or less inviting choices as night comes on. Then we move to stanza two, the sestet where, if we are trained sonnet readers, we can expect a development or shift, what we call the *volta*. The volta is often, in some way, the reveal, or the twist, or the appearance of the dove from the magician's hat. It is not the end, but a new beginning—something that we will want to solve, perhaps. How did this shift happen?

At this point in her poem, Stallings switches the focus immediately to sound rather than sight. *Focus* may not be the right word here, but I mean to convey a different kind of seeing. It is also turning up the volume. After all, by now the deepening violet has taken us into near total darkness. We might think of the stanza break as the moment where the evening grows so dark we are blinded to our surroundings. There is a shift in the way we must perceive things, so we will need to rely upon our sense of sound. In the sestet, sound takes over where sight leaves off. In the octave she has already mentioned the "new tunes," but remember that was related to visual movement. And the "song" of the bat is not the music of a bird, rather it is a kind of voice that gives us, beyond song, information. Sound in this first stanza is a kind of foreshadowing of what will happen more fully in stanza two. In the tradition of poetry, most poets relate the singing of the poet to the song of a bird—larks, mockingbirds, thrushes, ovenbirds—but never bats. Stallings is hearing (and seeing) things differently, as poets are known to do. Indeed it is one of the primary aspects of any poem to turn our emphasis from one way of perceiving to another.

Notice how Stallings uses not only the end rhymes to create a sonic repetition but also the repetitions of internal rhymes when she announces the songbird. In just these three lines beginning the sestet we hear an onomatopoeic play with how this songbird, "by rote" uses ornamentation: "sing…songbird…sings…song…song…rings." We can see that this, in all its complexity, goes well beyond ornamentation, while the poem is not devoid of that gift.

So many great poems are about poetry itself. We call this *ars poetica*. This poem is no exception. The poet is completely aware that her affinity is not only for bats but *with* bats, and for the way that they survive by feasting at night, locating their food not by sight, but sound. Perhaps this is indicative of the way the poet is able to find things in the dark that others cannot imagine. The first stanza allows the words to do double duty. A *glimpse* is a first sight of something that could be developed further. A *swallow* can be a bird, but it can also be the action of ingesting, nearly the opposite of a song that comes forth *from* the throat, not *into* it. "New tunes" are what the Modernist poet Ezra Pound suggested poets needed to put forth when he made his famous pronouncement. "Make it new," he said. Of course, many readers understand that a poem is "difficult to follow" due to its multiplicity of meaning and layers of perceptions and images. Poets perceive, much like the bat must be perceiving in lines six and seven, and a good poet goes through much "revising." Stallings is having some fun here with the notion of what it is to write (and read) a poem.

The poet, like the bat, makes sound but not just to hear herself. The poet makes this music to hear the thing the sound describes, the very shape of it, so that the poet can find what that thing is in the dark and either veer around it or consume it. If the thing to be perceived is finally internalized, it can then be made one with the poet. So many poets I know, when asked why they write poems, say things like: "to understand words better" or "to figure out what is going on in the world" or as I so often tell people, "to find out who I am." Putting words in the best order is similar to arranging molecules to make a better medicine or writing a more successful code for a more efficient computer program. We order the world to make life better. A poem does not just emote or express random feelings, though often we are taught this from elementary school to high school; it has to do with discovering how to live and be in the world. Just about any artist would admit this self-discovery as a purpose in making art.

As in Shakespeare's sonnets, the final turn happens in the couplet, though in Stallings's sonnet the last two lines don't rhyme. Still, they act as a turning point for a powerful final thought. Remember that the sonnet moved from sight to sound between octave and sestet. Now, within the sestet, between the first four lines and the couplet, the movement goes from making the sound to hearing it. This is the "last-minute pirouette" we might have "harkened" was coming if we had been paying close attention to line five. The echo has returned, finally, formally, strategically, geometrically, and we end by locating the exact shape of the thing: the sonnet. The formal shape of this poem cannot be emphasized enough.

Many readers unfamiliar with the finer qualities of sonnets might miss a thing or two, but that is not an insurmountable problem. Any art requires a breadth of knowledge of formal understanding to glean the most appreciation of the effects. It can be difficult, but you don't have to know everything to enjoy it. Line three's "difficult to follow," then, is not just the difficulty of our seeing the bats at night with their zig-zagging movements, but it also has to do with our understanding of good poems or even complex sentences strung across lines. If this is an *ars poetica*, we realize the poem has barely begun here in line three. It is, here, a "new tune," and the poet must be asking herself how she will arrive at her destination. That is a difficulty for the *writer*.

The difficulty for the *reader* is another thing. Some readers prefer a simpler poem of superficial feeling and sentiment. But this is never what we would ask of scripture, which we consider the greatest literature. Here's the British poet, Geoffrey Hill: "In my view, difficult poetry is the most democratic, because you are doing your audience the honour of supposing that they are intelligent human beings. So much of the populist poetry of today treats people as if they were fools. And that particular aspect, and the aspect of the forgetting of a tradition, go together." While not anywhere near as impenetrably allusive and arcanely historical as Geoffrey Hill's own poetry, the beautiful difficulty of Stallings's sonnet is something to be engaged, admired, and praised.

It should be noted that bats are not blind, only limited in their ability to see, especially at night. So we think of them as blind. Poets, seers in ancient literature, were sometimes portrayed as blind. Demodocus, the poet-singer in the Odyssey ("whom the muse loved above all others, though she had mingled good and evil in her gifts, robbing him of his eyes but granting him the sweet gift of song") is a blind seer. The irony is therefore rich in that, though he cannot see, the poet sees more of what has happened in past history, presently, and prophetically well into the future. Stallings doesn't go into it with any elucidation (the sonnet form doesn't have room, neither is it a Wikipedia entry), but we know that the echolocation the bat uses is a technique that will allow it to eat and survive. Without the aid of night vision goggles that humans might use, bats need some help locating insects in the pitch dark; and the use of vocalization and hearing function perfectly.

We read in the gospels how Jesus continually emphasized both the senses of hearing and of seeing to encourage His followers toward the kingdom of God. He healed both the blind and the deaf and often especially emphasized hearing. Eight times in the gospels, He says: "He who has ears to hear, let him hear." He knew that our earthly hearing and seeing are continuously fraught with error due to our fallen state, so the statement is not only encouraging but somewhat ironic. In Matthew 13:14, He quotes Isaiah and says: "'Hearing you will hear and shall not understand, and seeing you will see and not perceive." He understands that we might have glimpses of the truth, as Peter did when he called Jesus the Son of God, but then the world grows dark around us and we can end up in a place of blindness and denial. Peter later, staggering, even after he had seen the risen Christ, would need some night vision. He would need the light of the Holy Spirit and not just the light of day. The ear had to hear differently. The words had to shift: he would need to rely upon his calling, not as a fisherman, but as a fisher of men. Of course here, for the sake of linking us back to this poem, a poet myself, I'm playing with the word in Stallings's penultimate line, "calling."

Again, look at the diction in the sestet whose words have to do with sound: "sing," "songbird," "sings," "song," "song," "rings," "utterance," "harkenings," "calling," "hear," "voice." The sonic quality of the poem could hardly be emphasized more. The poem ends with the "shape of things," but this shape is arrived at through sound, not image. Surely, this is true of the way, at times in our lives when we can't see for the darkness around us, we can attempt to understand our predicament through listening. We must learn to see differently, via sound, or a different kind of sight. We might call that *faith* but not *blind faith*. A renewed way of experiencing the world might have a shape and a way of knowing more certainly than we might, at first, imagine.

***

One last note on the title: the word *affinity* is a word used to express a relation by marriage, as opposed to the word *consanguinity* (literally "with blood"), which would signify that "sanguine" relationship. Stallings doesn't pretend to want to be related to the bat by blood. Her speaker here is neither into the old Romantic songs of birds, nor the more recent romantic vampire craze, and certainly doesn't want to be bitten; rather, she desires to sing and be sung to, hearing some divine echo. She is brought into the family of these strange, winged creatures through a marriage, a pronouncement of words, an extended metaphor of sight and sound lodged within a mammal who has been given wings. An unlikely Pegasus, the bat here is a symbol of poetry itself. And the careful reader both sees and hears the difficult beauty.

Watching the Watch: Lisa Russ Spaar's "Watch"

Watch

Time, carnal cradle,
do we sleep in the feminine?

If so, why instead this casket
of sexless moonlight,

second hands gathering drams
of unspoken words,

the window's ladder of shadow?
Interior of the letter "O,"

tick of a starving dialect,
latch the bomb makes, nursing oblivion:

I am out-waiting them.
Pen scratch, carcass stalking

the diphthong hours of near-dawn,
is this suffering? I know

these instants until you arrive
as my rivals. Defeat them with your coming.

Critical of an all too easy poetry that seems to be popular and even de-manded these days, Geoffrey Hill wrote: "The craft of poetry is not a spillage but an in-gathering; relevance and accessibility strike me as words of very slight value. I have written elsewhere that *accessibility* is a perfectly good word if the matter under discussion concerns supermarket aisles, library stacks or public lavatories, but has no proper place in discussion of poetry or poetics." Hill, whom some have recently called "the greatest poet writing in English," died in 2016. He has written some of the most difficult poetry I have ever read. I consider myself a pretty good reader, but his work can be nearly impenetrable. I feel a great sense of achievement when I am able to come to terms with just a stanza or two.

I often argue that poetry should be difficult, and it rewards us more thoroughly when it challenges us. *No pain, no gain*, the old rhyme goes. I often give a provocative analogy to my younger college students to help them see afresh their college experience. It was once given to me from one of my own college professors, and it opened my eyes so much that I feel the need to pass it along. I tell them that the university is like a national park. At the visitor's center you will usually find a building with bathrooms and a gift shop, stuffed animals indicative of wildlife in the surrounding region, t-shirts, and smiling workers who can give you all the information about the park that you'd ever want. There are maps you can buy, and there in the center a 3D topographical map of the whole park you can peruse under plexiglass laid out on a sprawling table. There are a lot of visitors at the visitor's center. It can be crowded. But go out only a half mile on a trail in the national park and you are likely to be completely alone, except for a small flock of gray jays making a racket and perhaps some bighorn sheep that has strayed onto the path like a god.

It takes a little work (or a lot) to get out there, and you might be light-headed because of the elevation or even get altitude sickness from the strain and the unfamiliarity. Take water. Take a raincoat, a granola bar, and a map. Maybe do a few short hikes first. But if you push further, you will find yourself on top of a mountain, on top of the world, and closer to God. The university is like this. It seems to me that so many students filling out their degree plans might be like the lazy tourists walking around a visitor's center. They look for the path of least resistance. Hebrews 5:13–14 says: "For everyone who partakes only of milk is unskilled in the word of righteousness, for he is a babe. But solid food belongs to those who are of full age, that is, those who by reason of use have their senses exercised to discern both good and evil." I live in Texas, so I like the King James version better because it says "meat" instead of "solid food." The same notion about complexity and simplicity is true of poetry. There is a lot of accessible poetry available, but the meaty stuff requires effort. The payoff can be as serious as sharpening your skills in the discernment of good and evil. In our contemporary world where moral relativism has taken hold (or should I say, let go?), this effort should be something of interest to believers.

***

I want to take the time to look at a concise, but very difficult poem. Lisa Russ Spaar writes some of the best lyrically dense, difficult poems in America. Hers are not easily accessible poems; and I'm glad for that, perhaps in the way that I'm glad hiking to a steep peak in Northern New Mexico is not easy. If it were easy, I wouldn't be able to look across an entire range of mountains and valleys absent of human clutter. There is something nice about having an intensely beautiful space to oneself. Solitude, after all, is a much-needed place and state of spiritual meditation. Even God loves it: "And when he had sent the multitudes away, He went up on the mountain by Himself to pray" (Matthew 14: 23).

Some might think Spaar's diction is turgid, but the word *turgid* technically means swollen, and you won't find any inflated or bombastic phrasing in her poems. Carefully reading her, you believe each word choice has, if not at least one precise reason, a host of reasons to illuminate the world of her poem and the world beyond with yet another discovery. At times, you believe she might have cut the words out of the dictionary with a razor blade. And if you are reading one of her poems, go to the dictionary you will. As I do. The words in her recent book, *Vanitas, Rough*, are rich and difficult: *boscage, parousia, horaltic, hibernalphilia, niveous, byssal, trencher, brumal, ordure, regnant, augend, corms*...are just a few examples. Even if we know the meanings of these words, we want to look them up to find the etymological roots. This kind of linguistic and lyric intensity galvanizes Spaar's poems and is closely reminiscent of Hart Crane (along with his intractable optimism in the face of our [post]modern, crowded condition and solitary striving). What could become the ferocious striving of a poet like Sylvia Plath is transformed into a fierce abiding in Spaar's poems. Never pretentious, she delivers her choices via the context of beautiful syntax—a passion for the precision of the more arcane diction when it does appear.

In Spaar's short sixteen line poem "Watch," I believe she is at the height of her powers. A poem with a title such as this begins immediately with an intense complexity. We are invited to determine whether the title indicates an imperative or a noun or, likely, both. After all, poems tend to make the most of their meanings. The first sentence, a couplet, poses a very odd question addressed to Time. But before we can even get to that, we have had a revelation. The "Watch" we were wondering about is surely the noun, the thing that tells time, and yet it is quickly given an appositive, a renaming Spaar calls a "carnal cradle." A cradle rocks, of course, perhaps in a "tick tock" fashion, to help us get to sleep. But this is a *carnal* cradle—made of flesh. Mothers, these female bodies whose milk nourishes us during our first days, months, and years, these primary care-givers and sleep-rockers, seem to be addressed here. After all, who "watches" over us more than mothers? But could this "carnal cradle" be, as well, our own bodies? To be in a body is to be caught in time, to be restricted within a history and a bi-ography. But when we sleep and dream are we, via that dream world, able to escape the body imaginatively? The question is not only about the fem-inine or motherly aspect of time, but of how sleep works.

Who is the "we" here? Is it a royal we addressing the reader, or is "we" the speaker and Time, to whom she has already spoken? How can one "sleep in the feminine"? As opposed to the masculine? Is the "femininity" of sleep indicative of it being less strong, less masculine? At this point in the poem, we can't be sure. Nouns in other languages can have genders, but ours are mostly gender neutral. Is that what the speaker of this poem is asking us? Sometimes in poems, we have to suspend our understanding and continue reading, letting the context flesh out what a line or two might mean.

The next five lines ask another question. Here, it seems to me the speaker reveals something about insomnia: three images in a row. The "cas-ket / of moonlight" seems to me to be the rectangular shape the moonlight makes on the floor when it comes through a window. The "second hands" are the ticks of the clock on the wall, and the "window's ladder of shadow" is a further look back to the patch of light on the floor broken up by the grids of wood. The "why" of this sentence seems to me to ask why, instead of sleep, am I awake at this hour counting the seconds, staring at a ladder on the floor that offers me elevation to nowhere. The casket, the ineffectual ladder, the sexless moonlight (sexless in both the sense of unerotic and ungendered, companionless), and the unspoken words (the failure of poetry) add up to a great frustration for our speaker.

The next sentence brings us another series of images that work to create more frustration. She may have no words, but the "Interior of the letter 'O'" is a realization that even a letter can be hollow. The O is perhaps the opening of a mouth, the clock on the wall, or an exclamation or yawn, or most importantly, emptiness. The "tick of a starving dialect" is another failure of words, but notice how the poet gets it both ways: while she is complaining about not having words, she gets to pun on the word *tick,* as in the blood sucking arachnid. The next image is the "latch the bomb makes, nursing oblivion." This is a very difficult line, but you can make sense of it if you go back to that feminine imagery we understood from the beginning. Here a bomb is the thing nursing, latching on to its host, exploding with a tremendous suck of forgetfulness. Something tender is turned into something terrifying. This is quite a perfect image for insomnia where tender sleep, the infant rocking in a cradle, is exploded into a terrible wakefulness. And yet, the poet here in the next line claims, "I am out-waiting them." She is weathering the storm, trusting sleep will come. She will not be sucked into that interior of nothingness, but will "out-wait" the difficulty. How?

By finding words, by being a poet. The next image we get is "Pen scratch." We can understand this as the moment the poem begins for the insomniac speaker. No longer held helpless only in the moment of experience, she is able to find words as a kind of companion to help her make sense of things. She may not be fully herself, maybe only an unmoving "carcass," a trunk of a body, but she can imaginatively stalk "the hours," empowered now with a pen as her one limb for movement. She calls the hours she hunts "diphthong." I think this word refers to both the pronunciation of the vowel sound in the word "hours," but also the way "near-dawn" is multiple in its crossing over from the world of sleeping to waking.

W.B. Yeats, in *The Symbolism of Poetry*, suggests that "the purpose of rhythm is to prolong the moment of contemplation, the moment when we are both asleep and awake, which is the one moment of creation, by hushing us with an alluring monotony, while it holds us waking by variety." You can see that for the insomniac, this idea might become perverse. Rather than being rested and at the beginning of bringing the imaginative experience across that bridge from dream to reality, the insomniac is deprived of dream, only moving from the reality of dark to light, unable to find the imaginative dream state which is blessedly a rest from our rational searching.

But Spaar is not very reminiscent of Yeats. Spaar's most obvious forebear is Emily Dickinson. No poet should try to emulate Emily Dickinson, as idiosyncratic as that 19ᵗʰ century American poet is. If my injunction is true, it has something to do with the fact that Dickinson wasn't emulating anybody else. She was using a form of common hymn quatrain, but that's about where the influence of other poets ends. I warn other poets of Dickinson, yet the more direct influence on Spaar may emanate from her, our first lady of American poetry. Spaar does more successfully with Dickinson than any poet I can think of. The short phrases, the resonant abstractions, the sublime images, the slant and intense internal rhyme/alliteration, Death in the crosshairs, and the authority of mystery all work together in these poems, sometimes directly invoking Dickinson herself. When I think of what Geoffrey Hill said about "spillage and ingathering," I think of our beginnings in American poetry. Walt Whitman seems much more a "poet of spillage," of words sprawling across page after page in his life-long masterpiece, *Leaves of Grass*. Dickinson is the "poet of ingathering," of compact and intense spaces. I like to explain it to students in this way: our two earliest strong American poets are both like gunpowder. Whitman lights it on fire and spreads it across the sky: fireworks. Dickinson, however, jams the powder into a compact space, making a much more "powerful" poem we might think of as a bomb. Jokingly, I say, Dickinson is the bomb…but I mean it seriously, too.

Spaar's poems are not of the pyrotechnical variety. They are as brief and powerful as Dickinson's bombs. Dickinson was even more abstract, but beyond Victorian Romanticism and after Modernism, abstraction has its limitations. Spaar is aware of this. Nevertheless, I would argue that ultimately the poem here is about a big abstraction. *Sleep*, or the lack thereof, and then by association, *death*. Shakespeare, in his famous Hamlet soliloquy gives us the beautiful comparisons of death, sleep, and dream. We can recognize in Spaar's poem a flesh and blood battle with sleeplessness and the need for sleep and, I would argue, death. Wallace Stevens wrote in his poem, "Sunday Morning," that "Death is the mother of beauty." And that is from a man whose belief was secular, not religious. As Christians, we believe that you must die to be born again. Though death is the enemy, through Christ, the Word who rose again from the dead, we triumph over it. In Spaar's poem, insomnia is the enemy, but through the pen scratch, the word, she triumphs over it. Even though she doesn't sleep, she uses the lack thereof to get the poem written. The irony should be apparent: she is writing about the frustration of trying to write the poem: "drams / of unspoken words," yet here are the words on the page before us, the readers.

Notice that the "drams" might be mistaken for "dreams." And you don't need much. The word *dram* comes from a word meaning a small measurement of weight, especially used as an apothecary term. This is an essential few drops that can cure: poetry as healing medicine.

The last three lines of the poem can be read in a multiplicity of ways, but a primary reading I see is that "knowing these instants" is understanding the moments of wakefulness. The "you" addressed here must be Time who has been addressed directly from the very beginning. How can Time be plural, as rivals? Well, the ticking of the clock clearly can be understood as maddening to someone who can't sleep. But finally, this ticking must act, even through sheer exhaustion, as a metronomic pendulum that lulls the writer to sleep—to good sleep. The sleep of dreams and another world, another life. "Defeat them with your coming" then seems to me like the Savior's second coming, which is the final arrival, completing our salvation. We might normally fear death (or sleep from which we might not wake up), but with this presence of the "you" here sleeping alongside us, we might be comforted.

By the end of the poem, the title word *Watch* has been transformed from the instrument that tells time to the action of watching. The poet has turned the frustration of insomnia into the duty of a lookout. The word *watch* is used in the New Testament mostly in reference to the return of the Bridegroom or the end of times. When Jesus asks his disciples to pray with him during his dark night of the soul at Gethsemane, he tells them to "stay here and watch." But after a while he returns to find them sleeping. He gives them a warning: "Watch and pray, lest you enter into temptation. The spirit indeed *is* willing, but the flesh *is* weak." Yet they fall asleep again.

You can see the irony in relation to the Spaar poem. Her speaker *can't* sleep; the disciples can't help *but* sleep. In this way, though, because she can't sleep, the poet's words come alive to the page, and we're thankful.

Those of us who believe in the Word, and in second life, being born again, could certainly read the poem in this light. We've come full circle. The paradox is that the sleep of death allows us to embrace the true light of morning and realize our greatest dreams.

Spaar's poem might be difficult to understand, but consider the difficulty faced by the disciples to whom Jesus says: "Watch and pray, lest you enter into temptation. The spirit indeed *is* willing, but the flesh *is* weak." His disciples failed (a second time they fell asleep), but the Word ultimately prevailed. Of course, we know in that story that there was much more to come. A seeming nightmare was just beginning for Jesus and His disciples, but that greatest of difficulties would be overcome in due time.

The Supreme Absence:
Elizabeth Bishop's "The Moose"

The Moose

For Grace Bulmer Bowers

From narrow provinces
of fish and bread and tea,
home of the long tides
where the bay leaves the sea
twice a day and takes
the herrings long rides,

where if the river
enters or retreats
in a wall of brown foam
depends on if it meets
the bay coming in,
the bay not at home;

where, silted red,
sometimes the sun sets
facing a red sea,
and others, veins the flats'
lavender, rich mud
in burning rivulets;

on red, gravelly roads,
down rows of sugar maples,

past clapboard farmhouses
and neat, clapboard churches,
bleached, ridged as clamshells,
past twin silver birches,

through late afternoon
a bus journeys west,
the windshield flashing pink,
pink glancing off of metal,
brushing the dented flank
of blue, beat-up enamel;

down hollows, up rises,
and waits, patient, while
a lone traveller gives
kisses and embraces
to seven relatives
and a collie supervises.

Goodbye to the elms,
to the farm, to the dog.
The bus starts. The light
grows richer; the fog,
shifting, salty, thin,
comes closing in.

Its cold, round crystals
form and slide and settle
in the white hens' feathers,
in gray glazed cabbages,
on the cabbage roses
and lupins like apostles;

the sweet peas cling
to their wet white string
on the whitewashed fences;

bumblebees creep
inside the foxgloves,
and evening commences.

One stop at Bass River.
Then the Economies—
Lower, Middle, Upper;
Five Islands, Five Houses,
where a woman shakes a tablecloth
out after supper.

A pale flickering. Gone.
The Tantramar marshes
and the smell of salt hay.
An iron bridge trembles
and a loose plank rattles
but doesn't give way.

On the left, a red light
swims through the dark:
a ship's port lantern.
Two rubber boots show,
illuminated, solemn.
A dog gives one bark.

A woman climbs in
with two market bags,
brisk, freckled, elderly.
"A grand night. Yes, sir,
all the way to Boston."
She regards us amicably.

Moonlight as we enter
the New Brunswick woods,
hairy, scratchy, splintery;
moonlight and mist

caught in them like lamb's wool
on bushes in a pasture.

The passengers lie back.
Snores. Some long sighs.
A dreamy divagation
begins in the night,
a gentle, auditory,
slow hallucination....

In the creakings and noises,
an old conversation
—not concerning us,
but recognizable, somewhere,
back in the bus:
Grandparents' voices

uninterruptedly
talking, in Eternity:
names being mentioned,
things cleared up finally;
what he said, what she said,
who got pensioned;

deaths, deaths and sicknesses;
the year he remarried;
the year (something) happened.
She died in childbirth.
That was the son lost
when the schooner foundered.

He took to drink. Yes.
She went to the bad.
When Amos began to pray
even in the store and

finally the family had
to put him away.

"Yes ..." that peculiar
affirmative. "Yes ..."
A sharp, indrawn breath,
half groan, half acceptance,
that means "Life's like that.
We know *it* (also death)."

Talking the way they talked
in the old featherbed,
peacefully, on and on,
dim lamplight in the hall,
down in the kitchen, the dog
tucked in her shawl.

Now, it's all right now
even to fall asleep
just as on all those nights.
—Suddenly the bus driver
stops with a jolt,
turns off his lights.

A moose has come out of
the impenetrable wood
and stands there, looms, rather,
in the middle of the road.
It approaches; it sniffs at
the bus's hot hood.

Towering, antlerless,
high as a church,
homely as a house
(or, safe as houses).

A man's voice assures us
"Perfectly harmless...."

Some of the passengers
exclaim in whispers,
childishly, softly,
"Sure are big creatures."
"It's awful plain."
"Look! It's a she!"

Taking her time,
she looks the bus over,
grand, otherworldly.
Why, why do we feel
(we all feel) this sweet
sensation of joy?

"Curious creatures,"
says our quiet driver,
rolling his *r*'s.
"Look at that, would you."
Then he shifts gears.
For a moment longer,

by craning backward,
the moose can be seen
on the moonlit macadam;
then there's a dim
smell of moose, an acrid
smell of gasoline.

In general, poets are travelers. As with any vocation there are excep-
tions, but most poets I know travel a great deal. We're looking for input, a
way to see the world anew. Before poetry found its way to the page, we had
wandering bards who had to sing for their supper, and travel was essential
to them and their livelihood. This is an old story. Perhaps one of the oldest,

it is at the heart of one of the greatest poems ever written, Homer's *The Odyssey*. One of the primary themes in this epic is that, while adventures abroad abound, one would give up immortality to return home. While Odysseus revels in the tales of monsters, shipwreck, beauty, sports, battles, feasting, and encounters with the gods, he wants nothing more than to be home.

My own travels were limited when I was young. I grew up in a lower middle class family in Northwestern Pennsylvania. We took the annual summer trip to Delaware to visit grandparents, and occasionally we would venture somewhere further up or down the eastern seaboard. When I was fifteen, I went on a mission trip to Haiti that changed my life. I had never understood poverty until I experienced it firsthand in Haiti. While the rest of the mission team had a great time helping build an orphanage and minister to the sick (and it truly was a wild adventure to visit another country such as this), I can remember that I just wanted to go home. I was not a good traveler. In one way or another, we travel and come to an understanding of what home is. If we don't leave, we can never really know.

Jesus was almost constantly traveling during his lifetime of ministry. And it wasn't exactly comfortable, as he claimed to have "nowhere to lay his head." It should be obvious to anyone that his travel was more about giving than about taking. He spread the good news wherever he went, both in word and deed. And when he told his disciples (and by extension us) to "go into all the world," he meant to travel past Judea and Samaria, even "to the end of the earth." He had a worldwide perspective for himself and for us.

In recent years I've come to love the country of Spain, having taught in Seville a number of semesters abroad for Texas Tech University and once in Barcelona on a Fulbright Core Scholar Fellowship. Through learning more thoroughly the Spanish I barely understood in high school, becoming almost conversational by the end of each stay in Spain, I've learned a lot more about my own language. I actually wrote the bulk of this essay on Elizabeth Bishop while traveling in Barcelona because I was asked as a Fulbright fellow to give a few poetry lectures along with my teaching. I always become more objective about my home back here in Texas as a result of being away.

At some point, no matter how much my students have had their eyes opened to flamenco music, Gothic architecture, or amazing new foods, the students who travel along with me get homesick. They want that comfort only home can bring, whether that is Mom and Dad or Kraft Mac and Cheese. I'm the same way. I like lunch at noon rather than three hours later, and I miss even the smell of my house and especially my books. Elizabeth Bishop, in her poem "Questions of Travel," says: "Should we have stayed at home and thought of here?" Well, we know it's not that easy, though these days with Netflix and other streaming platforms we're easily transported elsewhere.

We've got to get some distance on things to get perspective. As for poets, it's not just home we want to understand, but we want to see things anew. Not just new things, but old things we have forgotten or misunderstood. A poem often reveals to us something that we already knew, but we never had exactly the right words for it.

More recently I've been spending my time abroad in Italy, hoping to write a book of poems about Italian culture, food, history, language, Rome, the island of Ischia, and so much more I still don't know. Being a traveler is very much about embracing the "not-knowing." You have to let yourself be vulnerable, and you have to make an effort at not being merely a "tourist." One of the major differences between being a tourist and a traveler is that one can see the tourist as a person who just comes in and plunders what he can get, while a traveler is a much more careful citizen—a student, thorough, patient, curious, self-aware, humble, who longs to be changed. The culture is more than a curiosity. And beyond being concerned with oneself, one gains greater empathy for others, having understood how they live and how they, too, are often thinking about what home is, much like Elizabeth Bishop.

***

The inaptly named confessional poets (Lowell, Plath, Snodgrass, Roethke, Berryman, and Sexton) have in common that their poems were more outwardly personal than the generations of poets before them. Often, the speaker in the confessional poem is recognizable as the poet him- or herself, sometimes blaming a father's failures rather than idealizing them or "confessing" anything to them in hopes of absolution.

Elizabeth Bishop stands apart from the most distinguished poets of her generation by instead searching in so many of her poems for her lost mother. Rather than employing blame or castigation or even damnation (See Plath's "Daddy" as prime example), many of Bishop's poems seem to be reaching out to her mother, or what she can recollect of her, and especially via the absence her mother leaves behind after her nervous breakdown, her confinement in a mental hospital, and death.

Bishop eschewed the confessional mode, believing this style all too personal (though in letters to him and to others she admitted Robert Lowell was the best at this kind of poem). But even he went too far in his later poems, she thought, warning Lowell about revealing too much that would be personally damaging. Bishop's poetry, on the surface, is always more emotionally restrained, but the family drama underlies a great deal of her poetry, and one of her best poems, "The Moose," though disguised with Bishop's demure and mannered verse, dabbles in the confessional mode.

Elizabeth Bishop had plenty of family tragedy with which she might make poetry. When she was eighteen months old, her father died. And by the time she was six, her mother, Gertrude, had been institutionalized in a sanatorium. Elizabeth was left in the care of various relatives until she went away to college. Bishop's short story "In the Village," published in her poetry collection *Questions of Travel* (1965), gives from a child's point of view a fictional rendering of her mother becoming incapacitated by grief and, thus, disappearing. In Lowell's *Life Studies* (1959), he too has a prose piece (presented as nonfiction), "91 Revere Street," about his parents, mostly focusing on their dysfunctional behavior, primarily his father's ineptitude. This prose piece colors Lowell's poems in *Life Studies*—encouraging us to use a psychological lens to read the other poems (one sees even the literary antecedents in Part III of *Life Studies* as dysfunctional poetic forebears). In a similar way, Bishop's short story casts a shadow on the poems following it in *Questions of Travel*. Since Lowell and Bishop were so close, it is likely that this technique of using the prose piece in the midst of *Life Studies* was an imitation of *Questions of Travel*. Beyond that, we know that "Skunk Hour" was written as a reply to "The Armadillo," both poems dedicated to the other poet.

Bishop writes in December 1956 to her aunt, Grace Bulmer Bowers, that she had composed "a long poem about Nova Scotia" and would dedicate it to her. Though "The Moose" was begun amid the poems of *Questions of Travel*, it would not appear until twenty years later. She would read it as the Phi Beta Kappa poem at Harvard University in 1972, then publish it in *The New Yorker*, and finally it would appear in *Geography III*. Due to the poem's beginnings in the mid-fifties, it is important to consider "The Moose" in relation to the poems of *Questions of Travel*, one of the most intricately designed poetry books of the last century. In it, the adventurous but awkward traveler, Bishop, sails to and through a new world while looking back (and forward), trying to understand what home is or might be.

The first section of *Questions of Travel* is entitled *Brazil*, and all the poems take place there. The poems in the second section, entitled *Elsewhere*, are poems where the travel is not to Brazil, but rather to Nova Scotia and back in *time*. These poems are dreamy divagations through Bishop's childhood, to the disappearance of her mother and the aftereffects of that absence. *Elsewhere* is framed with psychosis, beginning with the story "In the Village" and ending with "Visits to St. Elizabeth's." Both works confront madness, the former with a character very like Bishop's mother falling apart at the seams (she can't deal with a dress being made for her and, after her husband's death, becomes hysterical at the prospect of putting off her mourning clothes.) The final poem, "This Is the House that Jack Built," in a peculiar imitation of a nursery rhyme, illuminates Bishop's visits to Ezra Pound while he was institutionalized. The distance between the original nursery rhyme and Bishop's poem is the distance between home and mental home. Thus, *Elsewhere* begins with a prose scream and ends in a formally confined bedlam. For a poet as controlled and fastidious and mannered as Bishop, it is surprising to recognize the emotional horror involved in this framing, but certainly not the very meticulous framing itself. In fact, the first poem in *Elsewhere*, right after the story, is the innocently quiet poem, "Manners."

But "The Moose" would not find its place in *Questions of Travel*. Bishop could not satisfactorily complete the poem, and it would take around twenty years to finish, finally appearing in *Geography III* in 1976. As Helen Vendler observes: "Elizabeth Bishop's poems in *Geography III* put into relief the continuing vibration of her work between two frequencies—the domestic and the strange. In another poet the alternation might seem a debate, but Bishop drifts rather than divides, gazes rather than chooses" (Vendler 97).

Zachariah Pickard more recently describes Bishop's postmodern inclinations via her decentered subjectivity: "The single overarching proposal to which all of my arguments contribute is simply this: to begin with a perfectly useless concentration and end by sliding off into the unknown Is the fundamental pattern that underlies Bishop's art of description " (Pickard 5). While Bishop certainly admired this fundamental pattern in Charles Darwin's writing and imitated it, as Pickard points out, she does more than just slide off into the unknown. She makes discoveries and experiences epiphanies amid these mysteries, especially in her specific "questions of travel." Pickard's "decentered subjectivity" might simply be the old-fashioned use of the objective correlative which drifts into an even older negative capability.

Perhaps for Bishop, the perfect "perfectly useless concentration" is a careful look out the window of a bus moving through rural Nova Scotia at dusk. The first six sestets of "The Moose" each begin with prepositions or relative pronouns to keep the movement of travel going fluidly and relentlessly over these thirty-six lines.

> From narrow provinces
> of fish and bread and tea,
> home of the long tides
> where the bay leaves the sea
> twice a day and takes
> the herrings long rides,
>
> where if the river
> enters or retreats
> in a wall of brown foam
> depends on if it meets
> the bay coming in,
> the bay not at home;
>
> where, silted red,
> sometimes the sun sets
> facing a red sea,

and others, veins the flats'
lavender, rich mud
in burning rivulets;

on red, gravelly roads,
down rows of sugar maples,
past clapboard farmhouses
and neat, clapboard churches,
bleached, ridged as clamshells,
past twin silver birches,

through late afternoon
a bus journeys west,
the windshield flashing pink,
pink glancing off of metal,
brushing the dented flank
of blue, beat-up enamel;

down hollows, up rises,
and waits, patient, while
a lone traveller gives
kisses and embraces
to seven relatives
and a collie supervises.

The bus trip from Great Village to Boston would have taken nearly a dozen hours. Even the herrings of the first stanza are taking "long rides." The poem only gives us a portion of the first hour's journey. Bishop draws her reader to travel with her through the landscape of her childhood, letting us peer out the window at a kind of *paysage moralisé*. We move among the bay and tides from line 3 at "home" to line 12 "not at home." There is an underlying moral to this narrative and certainly a land of "the domestic and the strange." That strangeness extends from the simple peregrination of travel to the otherworldliness which appears in her more surreal poems like "The Monument" or "The Man Moth." The "fish and bread and tea" of line 2 seem fairly simple, but we should know fish and bread can be the stuff of miracles. Even Bishop in a very early poem, "A Miracle for Breakfast," turned coffee and a crumb into a kind of surrealistic landscape.

While the traveler in "The Moose" journeys through this landscape, constantly remarking upon the domestic (the bread and tea, the sugar maples, the farmhouses, the churches, the kisses and embraces of seven relatives, and even the herding dog), it should be noted that the bay, because of the tides, is just as often "not at home," and the bus ride is taking us away from Great Village where her mother grew up. There is a pastel beauty in the landscape of Bishop's origins (the red, silver, pink, lavender, and blue) but also a psychic distress. After that first period, the seventh stanza begins with "Goodbye" and a fog closing in, and darkness coming on.

In Robert Dale Parker's remarkable reading of "The Moose" in his book *The Unbeliever*, he observes that her passage through this landscape is a very close echo of Whitman's section 5 of "When Lilacs Last in the Dooryard Bloom'd." Just as his elegy for Lincoln moves descriptively through a grand and extended syntax across a multi-colored landscape finally arriving at the predicate "journeys a coffin," Bishop's poem carries us through a great deal of description before we see that "a bus journeys west" (Parker 125). The remarkable similarity here might lead us to believe we are in the elegiac mode.

We are driving to the interior, literally and emotionally, much like another of Bishop's poems, "Arrival at Santos." The next six stanzas take us through more of the domestic landscape of fog-draped flower and vegetable gardens and then through smaller villages where "a woman shakes a tablecloth / out after supper" as we surrender to the darkness.

> Goodbye to the elms,
> to the farm, to the dog.
> The bus starts. The light
> grows richer; the fog,
> shifting, salty, thin,
> comes closing in.
>
> Its cold, round crystals
> form and slide and settle
> in the white hens' feathers,

in gray glazed cabbages,
on the cabbage roses
and lupins like apostles;

the sweet peas cling
to their wet white string
on the whitewashed fences;
bumblebees creep
inside the foxgloves,
and evening commences.

One stop at Bass River.
Then the Economies
Lower, Middle, Upper;
Five Islands, Five Houses,
where a woman shakes a tablecloth
out after supper.

A pale flickering. Gone.
The Tantramar marshes
and the smell of salt hay.
An iron bridge trembles
and a loose plank rattles
but doesn't give way.

On the left, a red light
swims through the dark:
a ship's port lantern.
Two rubber boots show,
illuminated, solemn.
A dog gives one bark.

Though the setting is dark now, the domestic holds on. Another dog,
a symbol of fidelity and domestication, announces its presence. We have
been given one last glance at a small detail of the fisherman's boots via a

ship's lantern, and we move to the interior of both land (we have crossed the Tantramar Marshes) and the bus:

> A woman climbs in
> with two market bags,
> brisk, freckled, elderly.
> "A grand night. Yes, sir,
> all the way to Boston."
> She regards us amicably.
>
> Moonlight as we enter
> the New Brunswick woods,
> hairy, scratchy, splintery;
> moonlight and mist
> caught in them like lamb's wool
> on bushes in a pasture.
>
> The passengers lie back.
> Snores. Some long sighs.
> A dreamy divagation
> begins in the night,
> a gentle, auditory,
> slow hallucination. . . .

We have entered the bus which enters the woods and now we enter the dream world of the grandparents' conversation. This conversation takes us further into the realm of the domestic, but beyond that into Bishop's version of the confessional mode. The family tragedy begins to unravel:

> what he said, what she said,
> who got pensioned;
>
> deaths, deaths and sicknesses;
> the year he remarried;
> the year (something) happened.

She died in childbirth.
That was the son lost
when the schooner foundered.

He took to drink. Yes.
She went to the bad.
When Amos began to pray
even in the store and
finally the family had
to put him away.

Death upon death, alcoholism, sickness, shipwreck, moral decay, mental illness… The poem now abides under the spell of the moonlight. The lunatic in the poem is Amos, but we know that Bishop's mother was the one who had been "put…away." Plath and Lowell were more dramatic in their presentation of the confessional mode, the speakers of the poems hardly distinct from the poets themselves. But with Bishop also, the domestic world isn't all it's cracked up to be. As a matter of fact, when the moose appears a few stanzas later, we almost sigh with relief that wild nature has set up a roadblock to stop us, to save us from ourselves. Unlike the more severe confessional poets, we won't conclude the family gossip with a speaker who claims to "eat men like air" or who would complain, "I, myself, am hell."

"Yes . . ." that peculiar
affirmative. "Yes . . ."
A sharp, indrawn breath,
half groan, half acceptance,
that means "Life's like that.
We know it (also death)."

Talking the way they talked
in the old featherbed,
peacefully, on and on,
dim lamplight in the hall,

down in the kitchen, the dog
tucked in her shawl.

How similar that indrawn "yes" is to the tides of "the bay not at home": these tides controlled by the moon, the tides of alcohol, sanity, madness, of life and death. Yet again, a dog makes an appearance to bring serenity to the domestic scene. There is an expiation here in the confession of the familial sins, of having it out. The next three lines display the aftereffects of this catharsis, only to be ruptured by a near collision with the natural world:

Now, it's all right now
even to fall asleep
just as on all those nights.
—Suddenly the bus driver
stops with a jolt,
turns off his lights.

A moose has come out of
the impenetrable wood
and stands there, looms, rather,
in the middle of the road.
It approaches; it sniffs at
the bus's hot hood.

Towering, antlerless,
high as a church,
homely as a house
(or, safe as houses).
A man's voice assures us
"Perfectly harmless. . . ."

Some of the passengers
exclaim in whispers,
childishly, softly,
"Sure are big creatures."

"It's awful plain."
"Look! It's a she!"

Like those tides, the calm of the bus ride and the bedtime story don't last long, and the world shifts direction once again. As in Bishop's "Armadillo," the animal of the title has been withheld from us for most of the poem only to finally appear. The initial description of the moose is both strange and domestic: "high as a church, / homely as a house," the animal as both sacred and simple habitation. Most importantly, the moose is female: "antlerless," "It's a she!" The femaleness of the animal is signified by the lack of antlers and probably, upon further inspection, by the lack of male genitalia. This is a "she" by virtue of its absent parts. Helen Vendler compares with Bishop's moose, Frost's "great buck" in "The Most of It" as a male force of nature opposed to the human. In both poems, she points out, "Animal life is pure presence, with its own grandeur." In discussing animal life as a part of Bishop's poetry, Vendler notes that "Bishop's moose is at once maternal, inscrutable, and mild" (Vendler 110). I would argue that the inscrutability arises due to its identification with absence. In her essay on Bishop in *The Music of What Happens*, Vendler also suggests astutely that the death of little Cousin Arthur in "First Death in Nova Scotia" might very well be substituting for Bishop's father's death. This replacement in order to avoid the confessional is a kind of euphemism. Even in "The Waiting Room," the cry of her Aunt in the next room of the dentist's office becomes her own cry, or vice versa.

In fact, one of Bishop's most adroit skills is her use of absence as presence across her poems, especially in *Questions of Travel* and *Elsewhere*. The absence of the grandfather (and mother) in "Sestina" ultimately is the reason for the repeated tears in the poem. In "First Death in Nova Scotia," Cousin Arthur is present in body only; his absence predominates the poem and confounds the child speaker. And in "Filling Station," that somebody who "loves us all" is the absent mother of the poem, only present via the details of doily, begonia, and the orderly beauty of the filthy gas station—and via her dirty children, of course.

"The Moose," as well, makes astonishing use of absence. First, as previously noted, the absence of the moose's masculine physical features becomes the very presence of this looming female form. But also, as in

126

"Filling Station," we are given a picture of the family dynamic. On the bus we have a kind of surrogate family for this speaker: the grandparents, the fatherly driver, and the passengers who "exclaim in whispers / childishly." The only one missing seems to be the mother. This is also the case in "Filling Station," where we can "feel" this presence as a very physical sensation. Compare "Why, oh why the doily?" to Bishop's fourth line in the next stanza:

> Taking her time,
> she looks the bus over,
> grand, otherworldly.
> Why, why do we feel
> (we all feel) this sweet
> sensation of joy?

The answer to this "why" should be obvious. We have encountered the absent mother who has finally emerged "from the impenetrable wood," the *oscura selva* where Bishop had lost her way as a very young child rather than in mid-life. This moose in her sacred otherworldliness might very well be Bishop's Beatrice. Note that the moose does stand there "in the middle of the road" echoing Dante's "Nel mezzo del camin."

There is an obvious debt to the poet Wallace Stevens in this use of absence as presence. In a letter to Anne Stevenson, Bishop admits that Stevens was one of her earliest influences, though she later found him too romantic. Stevens' "Snow Man," at its conclusion, alerts us to "Nothing that is not there and the nothing that is." Or, as he says in the song of that mysterious "She" in "The Idea of Order at Key West": "The sky acutest at its vanishing" and ultimately those "ghostlier demarcations" that are the stuff of poetry. Surely, these two phrases apply to Bishop's epiphany:

> "Curious creatures,"
> says our quiet driver,
> rolling his r's.
> "Look at that, would you."
> Then he shifts gears.
> For a moment longer,

by craning backward,
the moose can be seen
on the moonlit macadam;
then there's a dim
smell of moose, an acrid
smell of gasoline.

Look back all you want, but the bus is moving forward again into the darkness. We can't live in the past and even the present draws us away into the future. While the end of the poem reveals that the human scent of gasoline overwhelms the dim and natural smell of moose, we have at least had a glimpse of the divine. As at the end of "The Waiting Room" where we are "back in it," we cannot remain in epiphany or revelation. Rather, we are in the human world where we have to travel on through the dark to our various destinations. This coda is slightly reminiscent and nearly as difficult as the end of Lowell's "For the Union Dead" where "the giant finned cars nose forward like fish…" Where Lowell is emotionally bitter, Bishop is merely portraying the literal acrid exhaust and reticently withholds emotional revelation.

The paradox of "The Moose" involves entering a world of darkness and absence where all we have are voices and memories. But we can still have otherworldly intrusions that allow us to see again, as if for the first time, even though our eyes have to adjust. And what is *not* there is as important as what is. We head off into the darkness again but not without hope. After all, this trip has just begun, and the travelers have many miles to go. The final stanza establishes a strong sense of closure with three pairs of rhymes instead of two.

In 1969, around the time Bishop is completing "The Moose," she writes a brief memoir of Marianne Moore. We know Moore was a model for her, a literary mother. Her emotionally-cool bestiary poems were powerfully influential to Bishop. In the memoir, Bishop admits to having a hard time concluding her thoughts and becomes playful:

I am turning the pages of an illuminated manuscript and seeing that initial letter again and again: Marianne's monogram; mother; manners; morals; and I catch myself murmuring,

"Manners and morals; manners *as* morals? Or it is morals *as* manners?" (*Prose* 140).

In the rear view of Bishop's final stanza of "The Moose," the last thing we see is the "moonlit macadam." Should it surprise us to have recognized this moose as mother?

Bishop does not cry out as her mother did; she finds a form. Though flirting with confessional poetry, her mannered verse would resist those moral risks that often came with confessional poets calling out family members whose actions could be emotionally devastating. She would opt for modestly hinting at a supreme absence. In this poem, her longing for her own mother is the most subtle cry one could imagine. Yet her "still small voice" speaks volumes about maternal love if we are listening carefully. And home, even through departure and the adventures of travel, though lost, through a strange encounter with wild nature, is paradoxically found.

Sure Measure:
Richard Wilbur's "A Measuring Worm"

A Measuring Worm

This yellow striped green
Caterpillar, climbing up
The steep window screen,

Constantly (for lack
Of a full set of legs) keeps
Humping up his back.

It's as if he sent
By a sort of semaphore
Dark omegas meant

To warn of Last Things.
Although he doesn't know it,
He will soon have wings,

And I, too, don't know
Toward what undreamt condition
Inch by inch I go.

People say that one of the problems of reading poetry is that we have
so little time in today's world. False. There is as much time as there ever
was. Twenty-four hours in a day. However, so many people, institutions,
networks, electronics, products, apps, and entertainments want our atten-
tion more than ever, and unless we take measures to defend ourselves, we

are going to fail under such constant assault. I'm as guilty as anybody—my smart phone buzzing, flashing, and pinging.

But poems are often very short, sometimes as short as the Richard Wilbur poem above, so you can read one quickly. False, again. Poems actually take a lot of time and concentration, and in a world where we are usually trying to multitask, this conflicts with what a poem requires: our full attention. A poem like "A Measuring Worm" might look like it would take two minutes at most to read, but maybe multiply those two minutes times ten if you really want to see what is going on. Or more.

Many distractions in life compete for our eyes and ears and souls, but there may be only one reason, and that is money. Because time is money. If someone has your time, they in some way have access to your wallet. The designers of phones and apps know this, and you have to know they are doing everything they can to keep you away from a life of solitude, paper books, or even prayer.

I don't allow the use of electronic devices in my classroom, because a video screen with its colors and noise will nearly always win someone's attention over words on a page. So, I tell students to put away their phones and only get them out if they need to look something up in relation to the poem at hand. "Have some manners," I say. Manners require an attention to detail, and the details of a poem will only be found with our full attention. Only ten years ago, back when mobile phones were a bit of a novelty, I told my students to not even bother bringing them to class. One day we were looking closely at a poem, and a student across the room yelped. At first, I actually thought someone was, in some odd way, excited about something in the poem (it's college; you never know). But, no—one of my students was having an epileptic seizure.

I jumped up from my chair, bounded across the room, and grabbed the kid before he hit the floor. He was jerking wildly and drool was dropping from the side of his mouth. Immediately, half the students in the class grabbed their phones and dialed 911. I was glad they had ignored my request to not bring their phones to class, because within five minutes campus police had arrived with the paramedics to get the student the help he needed. Needless to say, we didn't finish class. We were distracted.

***

Richard Wilbur, until he passed away in late 2017, may have been the greatest living poet writing in English. The publication of his *Collected Poems* in 2004 showed Wilbur to be the major poet we always thought he might be. While other poets throughout the twentieth century fled to the wilderness of fragmentation, wandered through the cities of common or uncommon prose, preached from the pulpits of free verse, and even abandoned the prisons of punctuation, he humbly continued the more "English" verse tradition passed down from Frost, Auden, and Larkin—a tradition that considered the iamb and rhyme still imaginative, vital, inexhaustible, and beautiful. Wilbur, in his best poems, conjures a cinematic and philosophical voice that is at once authoritative and decidedly curious. This kind of poetry demands no single style (though many dismiss it in the same way they might say that they don't like rap or country music, as if any given style is all the same), and Wilbur displays a range of formal expertise while retaining his particular voice.

Much of the literary criticism written about Wilbur's work concerns his attraction to manners, ceremony, and artifice. You can tell by his formal artistry that he is always conscious of his play. He is fastidious, though our egalitarian age often perceives this characteristic as a fault. A reader's perception of Wilbur varies, depending in what light that reader perceives the term *mannered*. Many think of someone mannered as someone supercilious or prideful, but this need not be the case. After all, manners are the measures we take to make others more comfortable. We say "thank you" and "please" and "Yes sir" to coordinate a more complete understanding of our social interactions. And by saying these things, we express humility rather than pride. A fancy table setting is not necessarily ostentatious; all those extra glasses, silverware, and plates are intended for the pleasure of the guest rather than the pride of the host. Admittedly, it may not always seem this way, and anyone can abuse something good toward ill purposes. Wilbur is not a fussy or careful poet. Rather, he is (to use phrases from his poems) a "suitor of excellence" and a "connoisseur of thirst." If manners are the more thorough actions we take to please others, then Wilbur is one of our most generous poets.

And he is, perhaps, our greatest contemporary poet of paradox. Wilbur's subject matter varies widely and he writes equally well on the great themes: art, history, love, war, death, dreams, nature, and theology. He is never merely witty, and he is as imaginative as Wallace Stevens, though quite different in his approach.

Wilbur's most widely known poem, "Love Calls Us to the Things of This World," is his best version of "in what manner the body is united with the soul." Wilbur is no ascetic: he gets to have his cake and eat it, too. And note, not "the World," but "This World." Richard Wilbur's very specific world is one that constantly comes to closure and grounding that occurs through cycles.

That poem was published early in his career in 1957. The book in which it appeared, *Things of This World*, won both the Pulitzer Prize and The National Book Award. Wilbur, unlike most poets for whom awards become distractions, continued to write strong poems throughout his career.

Even in a short, recent poem like "Crow's Nest," Wilbur transforms the natural world into the ship where the crow's nest becomes metaphorical. But that perch cannot remain metaphorical and beyond reach, where a competent poet might leave it. Wilbur circles back around to the real to move beyond mere competence. Where other poets settle into their metaphors, Wilbur resists closure until at least a cycle is complete. And the cycle is achieved through a variety of means beyond metaphor, such as movement through seasons, the course of a day, resurrection, and redemption. The closure is never absolute, as at the bottom of the page the paradox pulls us back up into the poem. One can see how Wilbur's formal tendencies lend him a helping hand (and foot): the rhyme and iamb are quite suited for the cyclical poem because these devices are cyclical and rhythmical in and of themselves.

While it is important to notice this cyclical movement, we see more apparently the way Wilbur can lead the reader by the eye and ear through very specific spatial movement in a poem. Notice how the senses and rhythms imitate the thing observed:

> More intricately expressed
> In the plain fountains that Maderna set
> Before St. Peter's—the main jet
> Struggling aloft until it seems at rest
>
> In the act of rising, until
> The very wish of water is reversed,

That heaviness borne up to burst
In a clear, high, cavorting head, to fill

With blaze, and then in gauze
Delays, in a gnatlike shimmering, in a fine
Illumined version of itself, decline,
And patter on the stones its own applause?

from "A Wall-Fountain in the Villa Sciarra"

Is there a more lovely, patient, vivid, exact, and formal description of water in American poetry? The further wonder of this description is that it refers to a completely different fountain than the title! Notice here how Wilbur slips beyond mere cycle or repetition and toward transcendence.

Wilbur often reminds us of another Christian poet, W.H. Auden. But while Auden's authority rises out of slightly more abstract and distant realms of meditation, Wilbur returns again and again to a more pastoral or domestic imagery (one might think of Frost, but the flora is more luscious, the waters more shapely, and the rooms more particularly well-lit). The quite cosmopolitan Auden is a man of the world, yet so is Wilbur. But where I imagine Wilbur amid the nature he describes, Auden views the same nature from the walls of the city or a train and through a cloud of cigarette smoke. In short, Wilbur is a much more privately personal than public poet.

Wilbur is one of the few American contemporary poets who professed to be a practicing Christian. Many of our poets who claim some kind of Christian worldview write much more about their doubts and reservations than beliefs. While Wilbur is no "inspirational" poet, his doubts or stumblings did not prevent his faith, humility, and passion from pushing through paradox, admitting to a higher beauty and order.

***

His poem "A Measuring Worm" was first published in *The New Yorker* magazine in February of 2008. At first it seems a trifling little poem of meager description, like many *New Yorker* poems. Immediately one notices that the title of the poem is not "An Inch Worm," though that is what we know we are observing. Wilbur emphasizes the word *measuring* to make us pay attention to that term. In fact, the word allows us to see the worm (and word) in motion, as a participle rather than the more static and firmly measured *inch*. The worm is observed initially in the act of "climbing."

Immediately, we see that the poem rhymes. Lines one and three create a kind of measured finality for each stanza with that sonic repetition. One can imagine the rhyming pattern as a kind of "measuring worm" crawling down the right side of the poem, the middle line bunching out much like the body of the worm, while the feet of the rhyming words are planted along the same line. There is a nice irony here in the movement of our eye down the page (in the pattern of the rhyme) while Wilbur has told us the caterpillar is climbing up.

The worm is described in the very first line as "striped," perhaps in the same way that a measuring stick or ruler is marked with stripes. He measures and yet is measured (we will see this is true of the poet/speaker later in the poem). The action of the inchworm "humping up his back" is described as "constantly" due to the lack of legs in the middle part of his body. If you look at an image of an inchworm, you can see it has five pairs of legs (three in the front and two in the back). Thus, the measure of the five stanzas is even more beautifully rendered. Could it be Wilbur's intention to mirror those arching legs with the arching of the five rhymes? Regardless, there it is. If we look at where that arch, or turn, comes in the poem, we see it is at the crux of the matter when this omega will "warn of Last Things." There are also the smaller arches between each pair of legs.

Just before this, at the very center of the poem we arrive at a crucial epiphany. The etymology of the word "semaphore" means "to carry a sign." This worm seems to be trying to tell the author something, and the poet realizes the shape of the worm is not just a hump. With his feet, his arched form makes the shape of an omega. *Omega*, we know, is the last letter in the Greek alphabet. From the last book of the Bible, we know that God is our "Alpha and Omega," our "Beginning and End," so here we have a signal, perhaps, from God (The "finisher of our faith") himself. This is confirmed in the very next line of the poem, with an eschatological warning of "Last Things." The words are capitalized in case we might not realize the gravity of the situation.

The worm here goes from being a kind of harbinger to being ignorant of its own situation: "he doesn't know it, / He will soon have wings." This prefaces the speaker's own realization in the last stanza, but before that happens, notice how the worm is referred to as "he" in the second line of this stanza, then "He" in the third. Of course, this is only an accident of the formal choice of capitalizing line beginnings, but it is nonetheless meaningful as we see the metamorphosis take place in both insect and pronoun.

Here at the end of this magnificent poem, a worm, which is nearly nothing, gains wings and becomes a butterfly. Then, metaphorically, and *metamorphically*, the worm and butterfly transform into a human being imagining his worm-like (read: mortal) state and the transformation possible. The paradox is extraordinary. Though the poem moves downward, it moves upward. Though all seems to point toward death, we understand via the visible world around us a type of second life. Though the speaker might move only inch by inch, he has made great leaps of understanding. Though the poem ends with this final stanza and a period, the last word of the poem is "go" which seems to signify something akin to the fact that we go away, as in "going, going, gone." It is a word of departure. Shortly before his death, Jesus explains to his disciples that he must leave them: "I go to prepare a place for you." However, "go" is also the evangelical word with which Jesus sent his disciples into the world to transform it.

The speaker says of the worm, "he doesn't know" and then of himself: "I, too, don't know." Ignorance is an inescapable condition, but it is also a prerequisite of humility and faith. A human's knowledge is always miniscule in the light of all human knowledge or what God must know. We should notice that Wilbur pushes this tightly controlled poem to have one last repetition via the sonic echo of alliteration or assonance in every third line: steep/screen, humping/his, omegas/meant, will/wings, and inch/inch. There is an inchworm-like bridge between these repeated sounds, for visual and musical effect. That final exact repetition of "inch" brings us to an extraordinarily tidy ending, perfectly measured. The paradox is rich. Despite the fact that we go "Inch" by "inch," we can surely make a great leap of faith. It will take a new body. With wings.

Wilbur's poems throughout his long career have almost strictly been created with the iambic line, but we don't see that in this poem. The lack of iambs in a Wilbur poem as the controlling foot is almost a shock. (One might even argue that the regular *foot* of the iamb is not in use here because the poem is about an *inch* worm, therefore a smaller unit of measurement, a syllable, is more appropriate.) When we look more closely, we can see that another form is in place here beyond the rhyme.

If we count the syllables, we realize that Wilbur has written a series of five haikus to make his poem. Lines one and three of each stanza have five syllables and each middle line is seven syllables. Wilbur used this rhyming haiku form a few other times in his career, first in a poem called "Thyme Flowering among Rocks" in his 1969 collection, *Waking to Sleep,* and then three other times later in his career with the poems "Alatus," "Zea," and "Signatures." Japanese haikus don't rhyme, but Wilbur's does, adding a challenge to the formal work. Although haikus are not made of iambs (the focus is on the syllabic count), notice that the poem ends with six iambs: "toward whát / undréamt condítion ínch by ínch I gó." Wilbur cannot easily shed the beautiful music of the standard foot in the English language, the iamb.

Traditionally, haikus are Japanese poems of the natural world that often emphasize a season of the year. We all know how seasons change, and the nature of transformation is a key to understanding many haikus. Obviously, in Wilbur's poem, the haiku is also about change and the awareness of the natural world, as well as its possibilities of showing us who we are or what we might become. We can see in this poem what was pointed out earlier about much of Wilbur's work: this emphasis on closure, and yet the paradox revealing that something closed has a way of opening again, through poetry.

***

Robert Hass, who edited *The Essential Haiku: Versions of Basho, Buson, and Issa,* says in his introduction to that book that the haiku form "was, from the beginning, very attentive to time and place." Wilbur's time and place in this poem are quite intimate and contained. The inchworm measures both space and time in this poem. As well, Hass claims that the haiku "required that the language be kept plain." In Wilbur's poem, only the word "semaphore" seems even slightly difficult, and the grammar is very straightforward. Hass points out another aspect of haiku that is interesting in relation to Wilbur's use of the haiku form:

> One of the striking differences between Christian and Buddhist thought is that in the Christian sense of things, nature is fallen,

137

and in the Buddhist sense it isn't. Another is that, because there is no creator-being in Buddhist cosmology, there is no higher plane of meaning to which nature refers. At the core of Buddhist metaphysics are three ideas about natural things: that they are transient; that they are contingent; and that they suffer.

Wilbur, being a Christian poet, gets it both ways, it seems to me, in his use of a form connected with Buddhism. Readers of this poem are not as concerned with the worm (as representative of nature) being fallen, so that issue falls to the wayside; we are concerned about the fallen nature of the speaker who confesses: "And I, too, don't know / Toward what undreamt condition / Inch by inch I go." In Judeo-Christian belief, to be fallen is to be cursed with a death sentence. Yet, for the Christian, death will ultimately be "swallowed up in victory." The final word "go" is one of movement—a movement upward, beyond the poem, with wings.

As Wilbur points out, the caterpillar doesn't know his own condition. But we, with a God's eye view, outside of the worm's confines of space and time and limited intellect, surely do. We can extrapolate this transcendent potential to the human condition and its limitations in time. Our own steps are limited. Not only do we not fly, but in later life—in old age—our steps begin to shrink. The haiku exhibits this form of growth—but also shrinking. Nevertheless, for the Christian, we believe in a resurrection not only of the soul but of the body. The risen Christ in his new body was apparently able to fly through walls and ultimately ascend into the air, and perhaps this is the metaphor we can imagine for our own resurrected body after death that moves from legs to wings, from steps to flight.

Most anyone recognizes that a worm is synonymous with death. When we die, if we are put into the ground, the worms eat us, and our bodies return to mere soil. To say then, "a measuring worm" is even more significant. We can measure ourselves by the worm's actions, its shape, and its purpose. Although inchworms do not eat human flesh, we know that other worms do, and the poet is conscious of this. In the end, the real worm that measures who we are is not some cute little inch worm on a window screen, but the maggot who reminds us that our lives are but for a moment and that we are, in many ways, hanging by a thread. Despite this, the inchworm is harmless, and perhaps in the scope of eternity the Christian poet might see death this way.

The fact of the window screen is important. It lets us know we are between two worlds, inside and out, but also between the worlds of life and death. It is reminiscent of Emily Dickinson's famous "I heard a Fly buzz" in this way, in that the insect's placement upon the window is pregnant with spiritual meanings. With a screen rather than a window, the air (or spirit) can move freely between two worlds, though the body cannot.

The Apostle Paul writes in I Corinthians 15: 19 that, "If in this life we have hope in Christ, we are of all men most pitiable." Many versions translate that last word as "miserable." In Wilbur's poem the idea that, finally, the wings of another life await us is not just a metaphorical dream to the Christian. It is a spiritual reality that gives us hope beyond what we can measure in the here and now.

***

It is October 15, 2017. I have just learned that Richard Wilbur has passed away at the age of 96 years old. I feel an enormous sense of loss now, knowing that he will not write any more poems. I was blessed to have met him a few times: once in a graduate poetry workshop where he visited us in Gainesville, Florida, and once at the West Chester Poetry Conference where he and I chatted briefly about haikus, strangely enough.

One of his great poems, "Year's End," is a gorgeous meditation on death much longer than "A Measuring Worm," though I think both are equally rich in how they address death directly, without fear. Its last stanza begins, "These sudden ends of time must give us pause." Wilbur's lines, often end-stopped or taut with meaning (each functioning as coherent units of meaning), are full of these pauses, more so than just about any contemporary poet. Each line ending, often enforced by rhyme, helps us slow our pace. Why rush to our deaths? Why not pause? Even if to meditate on death? And life. The last two words of "A Measuring Worm" are "I go," signifying both death and life. Richard Wilbur may be gone, but his poems go forward with us, keeping him right here where we need him.

Honesty in the Shadow of Faith: Philip Larkin's "Church Going"

Church Going

Once I am sure there's nothing going on
I step inside, letting the door thud shut.
Another church: matting, seats, and stone
And little books; sprawlings of flowers cut
For Sunday, brownish now; some brass and stuff
Up at the holy end; the small neat organ;
And a tense, musty, unignorable silence,
Brewed God knows how long. Hatless, I take off
My cycle-clips in awkward reverence,

Move forward, run my hand around the font.
From where I stand the roof looks almost new—
Cleaned, or restored? Someone would know: I don't.
Mounting the lectern, I peruse a few
Hectoring large-scale verses, and pronouce
'Here endeth' much more loudly than I'd meant.
The echoes snigger briefly. Back at the door
I sign the book, donate an Irish sixpence,
Reflect the place was not worth stopping for.

Yet stop I did: in fact I often do
And always end much at a loss like this,
Wondering what to look for; wondering, too,
When churches fall completely out of use
What we shall turn them into, if we shall keep
A few cathedrals chronically on show,

Their parchment, plate, and pyx in locked cases
And let the rest rent-free to rain and sheep.
Shall we avoid them as unlucky places?

Or, after dark, will dubious women come
To make their children touch a particular stone;
Pick simples for a cancer; or on some
Advised night see walking a dead one?
Power of some sort or other will go on
In games, in riddles, seemingly at random;
But superstition, like belief, must die,
And what remains when disbelief has gone?
Grass, weedy pavement, brambles, buttress, sky.

A shape less recognisable each week,
A purpose more obscure. I wonder who
Will be the last, the very last, to seek
This place for what it was; one of the crew
That tap and jot and know what rood-lofts were?
Some ruin-bibber, randy for antique,
Or Christmas-addict, counting on a whiff
Of grown-and-bands and organ-pipes and myrrh?
Or will he be my representative,

Bored, uninformed, knowing the ghostly silt
Dispersed, yet tending to this cross of ground
Through suburb scrub because it held unspilt
So long and equably what since is found
Only in separation—marriage, and birth,
And death, and thoughts of these—for which was built
This special shell? For, though I've no idea
What this accoutred frowsty barn is worth,
It pleases me to stand in silence here;

A serious house on serious earth it is,
In whose blent air all our compulsions meet,

Are recognized, and robed as destinies.
And that much never can be obsolete,
Since someone will forever be surprising
A hunger in himself to be more serious,
And gravitating with it to this ground,
Which, he once heard, was proper to grow wise in,
If only that so many dead lie round.

Until Covid-19 slowed the world to a crawl last spring, it seemed that every month or week we heard in the news about another terror attack, by either someone from a radical Islamic faction or just another American citizen with a pile of guns at a school. The psychology, mental defects, personal suffering, loves, hates, failures, beliefs and history of any person are a complicated wonder amid circumstances. Though we try to assess blame and pronounce judgment (and must try for justice's sake and our own belief that the world should make some sense), ultimately it's complicated. We might want a simple and immediate solution to our tragedies, but we should know better. It takes time. We realize this lack of an answer is of little consolation to the victims of tragedy.

People often turn to poems in times of distress. Great poems are never ultimately simple and do not offer simple answers, rather they show us the beautiful complexities of language and meaning. After September 11, 2001, a number of poems were circulating: Auden's "September 1, 1939," Wislawa Szymborska's "The Terrorist, He Watches," and E.A. Robinson's "The House on the Hill." Not long after the dust had settled from the collapse of the Twin Towers, I remember sharing a different Auden poem that immediately came to my mind, "A Summer Night." While I also shared meaningful scriptures of encouragement with my friends such as "The light shines in the darkness, and the darkness did not comprehend it" (John 1:5), I realize secular poems are necessary and helpful with living in the world. Even Paul, in his rhetorical preaching on Mars Hill, shows an awareness of secular culture and invokes the power of art to persuade and give meaning to our lives.

In times of duress people turn to prayer for answers, more often than they do to poems. Even if that prayer is only the invocation of the name of God; prayer not only to reach out to God for immediate help to save, but also prayer to help the afflicted find words because that is the way we grieve and heal. We do not grieve only with indistinguishable cries or howls (though sometimes that is the case), but with words. Words, despite what some postmodern theorists suggest, *do* have meaning. The word *mean* actually *means* "middle ground." The middle ground of what? I would argue that the meaning word *do* is the middle ground between the physical world and the metaphysical. Words are our bridge to heaven, to paradise, to the otherworldly, and we need them. Creation is spoken into existence via the Word, and from existence we reach back to the Creator with words. Words are our connection with the divine. Mix them with the mystery of song, and perhaps we end up on the divine side of this bridge.

Words also "mean" between people. They function as a kind of magnetic middle ground that draws us together. Without them we might know a physical attraction, but we ultimately need words. Even lovers, when they have consummated their relationship, ask, "What are you thinking?" Cigarettes aren't enough. That bridge of language obviously need not be erotic, but it is the source of an exchange of love, creating a relationship. Both can't talk at once and communicate. One must talk, and one must listen, in turns. The act of listening lovingly sacrifices my mouth for my ear. God creates the world with words. Genesis 1 and John 1 attest to it.

I am interested in two words, a phrase, that I came across in the evening hours after a recent mass-shooting: *prayer shaming.* The phrase appeared in a brief article posted online by *The Atlantic* a little while back. I see this shaming happening before my very eyes whenever national or international tragedy strikes. Some friends express their grief through tweets and Facebook posts by suggesting that people not pray, but act. "No more thoughts and prayers," they say. We need to change the laws of the land (specifically, gun control) that allow and even encourage these heinous acts. They believe this as if prayer were mutually exclusive from action. After the San Bernardino terrorist attack, *The New York Daily News* headline read: *God Isn't Fixing This.* The simplistic notions of the problem of evil rose again before us to accuse believers, asking, "Where is God?" In my own prayers yesterday morning, after reading scripture, I prayed over what Jesus said, "Do not judge lest you be judged." Because I had meditated on these words, they came back to me, and I didn't lash out against the unbelievers who seemed to be lashing out. Because of my own prayer, I realized that this crying out against God is a kind of grieving as well. I don't believe that prayer makes God do something; prayer changes *me*. For the better, I believe. If we believe James 5:16, that "the effective, fervent prayer of a righteous man avails much," we should determine not to be prayer shamed.

***

One of Philip Larkin's most famous poems is "Church Going." The centerpiece of Larkin's second collection *The Less Deceived*, this poem portrays a speaker who expresses very clearly his skepticism of religion and yet finds himself curious as to why others have found or still might find an interest in a church, and not just an historical one. His biographer Andrew Motion calls the poem "an elegant archetype of his tone, method, and interests" and describes its "self-mocking, detail-collecting, conversational manner" typical in so many of his poems. Despite the poem's mockery of the faith, I know a number of Christian poets who consider it among their favorites, admiring the verse for its careful form, intense thoughtfulness, and subtle wit. To any of us "poet-believers," Larkin's poem might seem very much like a kind of reluctant and irreverent prayer. Josh Larsen writes in his book *Movies Are Prayers*:

> Let's accept that prayers can be unintended and can come from unbelievers, that even the howl of an atheist is directed at the God they don't acknowledge. In this way, we can explore movies anew. Films are not only artistic, business, and entertainment ventures, they are also elemental expressions of the human experience, message bottles sent in search of Someone who will respond.

So it may well be with poems. "Church Going" seems at first to be merely a poem that comically (and seriously) makes fun of a disappearing faith as evidenced by an empty church in rural England. Two hundred years before this poem was written, the Great Awakening had moved from America to England, and a blazing growth of Christian belief spread through England through men such as John and Charles Wesley. Larkin's deserted church shows that the embers have nearly died. The speaker's visit to this building is one of mild curiosity and an outright denial of any sort of devotion. He likely has been riding his bike through some countryside and on a whim decided to stop to have a look.

From the beginning, language is at play. Even the title "Church Going" works on a number of different levels. This man is "going to church" only in the most secular of ways—to look at its details and significance through a historical lens.

> Once I am sure there's nothing going on
> I step inside, letting the door thud shut.
> Another church: matting, seats, and stone
> And little books; sprawlings of flowers cut
> For Sunday, brownish now; some brass and stuff
> Up at the holy end; the small neat organ;
> And a tense, musty, unignorable silence,
> Brewed God knows how long. Hatless, I take off
> My cycle-clips in awkward reverence,

The speaker is an agnostic man who doesn't want to mix with the worshipful. He begins by making fun with little slights: viewing this as just "Another church," referring disingenuously to prayer books as "little," ignorantly calling the accoutrement of worship "brass and stuff," ironically labeling the altar "the holy end," using "brewed" to conflate religious belief with perhaps any superstitious kind of witch's cauldron or even beer-making, and removing his cycle clips as a kind of mock reverence. Later he will call the church an "accoutred, frowsty barn." All these phrasings laugh at religion; and yet he admits the silence is "unignorable," and something compels him to look and listen: "Yet stop I did, in fact I often do / And always end much at a loss like this." He is trying to understand what draws him to a place he doesn't believe in. Poetry always pays tribute to the complexity of an issue, no matter what the assumptions may be. It is not dogmatic and tends to walk a line between possibilities. Yeats stated that "Of our quarrels with others we make rhetoric; of our quarrels with ourselves we make poetry." In Larkin's poem, this assumption that religious belief has died just isn't going to provide for a very good poem. Rhetorically, he could make his point, but the speaker isn't satisfied only to pronounce the death of belief, no matter how evident it might seem. If he is writing a poem, he has to ponder the mystery.

145

As well as this initial linguistic play on "going" (going into a church building), the phrase "church going" is further understood as *dying*, as in "going, going, gone." To enact this very notion a little later in the poem, in stanza 4, the poet will use "go on" and "gone" in its rhyme scheme. The first line of the poem, "Once I am sure there's nothing going on" has even more fun with the idea of going, as in something *not* "going on" or occurring. The iambic pentameter of the line sets the pattern, and the final foot of the first sentence (a spondee), "thud shut," enacts the finality of the door closing dramatically, as if this might be some kind of haunted house. You can almost hear the echo of it reverberating in the empty space at the end of the line and in the physical space of the church. There is a ghost of something here, and the speaker, while making fun of the place, will try to understand it and speak to it. The flowers are "brownish" indicating decay, yet their presence indicates that someone brought cut flowers recently. The silence speaks to the fact of the church's emptiness, but it is "unignorable." Why so? The poet/critic Stephen Burt recently said in one of contemporary poetry's most-viewed TED talks: "We're all going to die — and poems can help us live with that." I have to agree. To the speaker of "Church Going," death might be the only reason the church is ultimately necessary.

Can a poem of unbelief be more laden with an experience of God than a more intentionally "inspirational" poem aimed at glorifying Him? The believer might wish it were not so, but she must see how often Jesus revealed the beauty of his message through paradox. We know that in suffering we can experience God more fully than in times of peace and ease. We understand that when we are weak, we are strong. Can doubters (good ones) doubt beautifully? Certainly, we all doubt. Even evangelically—how might believers come to understand those who can't seem to relay the faith that we have so gracefully experienced? How do we connect with them? Might we sympathize with their doubts? Ultimately, the difficult realities of suffering and death need answers, and the church's answers might be of interest to any mortal. Larkin's self-deprecation allows him a kind of humility from which most boastful "inspirational" poems would benefit. We can see that he is honestly asking questions in how he moves from pride to humility. He says, "Someone would know; I don't," and "I wonder," and "I've no idea" and admits he's "at a loss."

The transition from the penultimate to the last stanza is one of deepening sincerity. All mockery is left behind. Larkin quickly goes from recognizing the church as a "frowsty barn" to understanding it as a "serious house." How has this architectural imagining shifted? Jesus's own birth was humble enough—shepherds found him lying in a manger. His subsequent rise to teaching in the temple and his recognition as "King of the Jews" reveals a startling shift in the architecture around him. But Larkin doesn't specifically turn to the person of Jesus to finish his poem or fall on his knees to worship. It seems that he steps outside the church.

It might not be apparent to an untraveled reader that country churches in England are often adjacent to graveyards. This is certainly the case here, where in the final lines the hunger for seriousness is explained by "gravitating with it to this ground, / Which, he once heard, was proper to grow wise in, / If only that so many dead lie round." The speaker has moved beyond the interior of this "special shell" just outside the door. The ground is the soil in which we are buried. The "*grav*itating" is the pull of the grave. We die, and the naturalist's view only offers cold comfort: we're food for worms or perhaps some vague notion that our energy is added back into the cosmos. Yet the church tells a different story: our lives are not over when we die. We have a soul that continues and even flourishes after death. According to his biographers, Larkin was terrified of death. So many of his poems bear witness to that fear.

Early in the poem, the speaker mocks preaching and the scriptures by standing on the dais, pronouncing: 'Here endeth'. A few lines later his imminent departure from the church results in an "end much at a loss like this." Two stanzas later he wonders who "Will be the last, the very last, to seek / This place for what it was." Notice the obsession with finality, as if he senses an end to humanity's belief in God that will be absolutely final. "Church Going" was published in November of 1955, in the early days of the Cold War when the threat of worldwide nuclear annihilation hung in the air. Just a year later, Nikita Kruschev would say to a NATO envoy: "We will bury you."

Larkin mentions in the final stanza the word "serious" three times. A poet's repetition of a word is always important, and Larkin might have known the etymology of *serious* traces back to Germanic roots meaning *grave* or *heavy*. Yet, in the final stanza Larkin allows his speaker, because of this seriousness, a more faithful possibility of something such as "destinies."

147

Not just a single destiny of the grave. He says: "And that much never can be obsolete, / Since someone will forever be surprising / A hunger in himself to be more serious." That "forever" hints at something beyond, does it not?

We hope to die more peacefully than in some terrorist attack surrounded by hatred rather than love. But still, we die. Our "special shell" may crumble, but those of religious belief (and even those who doubt) know something serious is going on, and perhaps only the mystery of poetry can help us understand it. While Larkin surely pokes fun at belief and may seem to dismiss the faithful as mere relics of a former time, it is clear that the poet feels a kinship with them. His craft of finally and wonderfully slant rhyming "surprising" with "to grow wise in" is quirky and comedic, but note how the conclusion of the rhyme is the more serious half. As Robert Frost suggests, the figure of a poem "begins in delight and ends in wisdom." Frost also says, "The figure is the same as for love." Anyone's desire is ultimately satisfied in something more than the pleasure of silliness or nihilism; we hope, at least, for wisdom or love.

And very much like Frost, Larkin's poetry is strictly formal, but natural and not stilted; it is rhetorically convincing and yet it allows for mystery. This entire poem is written in the measure of iambic pentameter, rhyming, and still the poem seems naturally spoken: a difficult achievement. The artifice is high, but the speech seems conversational, as if anybody might be telling you his thoughts about what he did one afternoon. This formality might even be said of the Anglican church building, the liturgy, and even the orderly graves: though they serve the purpose of communicating the message of the gospel (of life and death) in clear terms, these are all artificial and ceremonial structures that go beyond utility. At its heart, English is highly iambic due to the nature of our vocabulary, grammar, and syntax. One might argue that belief, at its core, is natural and not the phony religion the speaker seems to suggest he understands early in "Church Going." The chaos of death and the fear that comes with it might be overcome by the order of meaning and love, even if that meaning is limited by doubt. And art, with its own order and voice of recognition, provides a kind of solace.

I finished the first draft of this essay a week after a Texas Tech student shot a police officer in the head just a few blocks from my house. My children, wife, mother-in-law, and I waited for a few hours on pins and needles until they caught the perpetrator. We were helpless to do much of anything, but we prayed together. My prayer was not eloquent. It was not a poem, but it was essential to find words and to connect through those words to a good and living God, a God of mercy and grace. It brought a measure of peace to us. And I will have to, again and again in this broken and hurtful world, as a poet or as a regular citizen, find words for this seemingly endless violence and death, trying to find some solace, wisdom, serenity, or maybe just the words that can take the place of my frustration and anger, my fear and heartbreak, my doubt.

When Opposites Attract:
Geoffrey Brock's "Exercitia Spiritualia"

Exercitia Spiritualia

We met, like lovers in movies, on a quay
Beside the Seine. I was reading Foucault
And feeling smart. She called him an assault
On sense, and smiled. She was from Paraguay,

Was reading Saint Ignatius. Naivete
Aroused her, so she guided me to Chartres
And Sacre Coeur, to obscure theatres
For passion plays – she was my exegete.

In Rome (for Paris hadn't been enough)
We took a room, made love on the worn parquet,
Then strolled to Sant'Ignazio. Strange duet:
Pilgrim and pagan, gazing, as though through

That ceiling's flatness, toward some epitome
Of hoped-for depth. I swore I saw a dome.

For most of the world, football is a game in which players kick the ball
strategically around a large grassy area and, ideally, into a goal at one end
of the field. In America, football is a sport in which the foot rarely touches
the ball. And when it does, we see this action as a failure to accomplish
more. There are so many varieties of the game, spectators need to know the
context to be sure of the rules: professional, college, Canadian, arena, etc.
Ask those who play or watch these versions of the sport, and they will detail

for you the aesthetic beauty and strengths of each. But the fact remains that the foot does not often touch the ball. This does not necessarily make our football inferior, of course. But we Americans like to think we're different. We call soccer what most of the world knows as football.

So it goes with the sonnet in America, and elsewhere: eighteen-line sonnets, dream songs, twelve-line truncations, fourteen-line blank verse poems, all the way to free verse prose poems that the author entitles "Sonnet" or declares a sonnet because it "feels like a sonnet." A few years back, some poet was writing "disheveled" sonnets. The word *disheveled* sounds much more distinguished than *incompetent* or *ham-fisted*. Actually, "incompetent sonnets" might be useful. This way, you could blame any verbal failure on the poem instead of the poet. Readers of poetry know that *sonnet*, in the simplest etymological sense, means only "little song." Even so, most sonnets are rigorously structured. While contemporary experimentation with the form enlarges our poetry, and while playful reactions to older and stricter forms open up new possibilities for our poetics, poets (those who care most about how words mean) should wonder about the name of the game.

Most often a sonnet can be identified by shape. Its familiar form is often, visually, the shape of a piece of paper or a handkerchief, most of the time slightly longer than it is wide. If the poem has a break between octave and sestet, it often resembles the visual weight in some Mark Rothko color fields, one larger rectangular block floating above or under another. The word *line* comes from the Latin *linea*, or thread. The word *text* is clearly at the root of *textile*, which is a plurality of these horizontal threads (lines) interwoven as one moves down the page by vertical threads of sound, meaning, rhyme, grammar, and syntax. The colorful patterns formed in the sonnet as a result of these interweavings reveal the personality, style, and the formal manners of each poet.

***

From the Renaissance until the 20th century, the theme of the sonnet most often concerned erotic love. Such is the case with Geoffrey Brock's poem, "Exercitia Spiritualia." I knew Geoff from the University of Florida, where we were poetry students together. He had already taken a Ph.D. in comparative literature from the University of Pennsylvania, and he had come back to school to study for the M.F.A. as a poet rather than a scholar. If this didn't intimidate us (it did), we also discovered Geoff was publishing translations of Italian writers. It was daunting to be in the same classes with him, to say the least.

Perhaps it is worth mentioning that revered critic and poet Ron Silliman once lumped Geoffrey Brock into a group of poets whom Silliman calls the School of Quietude. He means it as an insult (suggesting that ten-year-olds regularly write better poetry than these folks) and particularly would insist that poets in this so-called school don't make any music or meaning that matters to the contemporary poetics that Silliman promotes. When one sees the kind of stunning craftsmanship achieved in a poem like "Exercitia Spiritualia," one might wonder who is this Ron Silliman? Well, he is a critic/theorist/poet who recently proclaimed that in his work "every sentence is supposed to remind the reader of his or her inability to respond." Talk about quietude. At one point back in 2005, Silliman admitted on his blog that Geoffrey Brock's "Exercitia Spiritualia" was a poem worth reading, though he didn't go into any detail about the beautiful complexity of the poem.

Of course, the sonnet began long ago as an Italian form, so knowing Italian can only benefit the writer of sonnets. Giacomo de Lentini, a 13th century poet, is the first known sonneteer. Soon the greatest of poets, Dante Alighieri, was writing them. There is no other traditional form as prominent as the sonnet. While sestinas and ghazals seem to be all the rage these days, we still see more sonnets. And the sonnet has had a continuous development and presence since Dante. Brock's practice with Italian and with traditional forms results in an astounding specimen. The sonnet is known for changing through the years, developing new strategies and rules while its practitioners work within (and beyond, often unfortunately) the confines of a rhyming, 14-line iambic pentameter poem. But the sonnet is known for its changing landscape, and any poet wants to be the author of some new and brilliant sonnet invention.

One sees immediately Brock's variation: the rhyme is eye rhyme rather than aural rhyme. "Quay" (pronounced KEE) does not quite rhyme with "Paraguay." And the French theorist "Foucault" certainly does not rhyme with "assault," though the speaker's lover certainly links these two words as a straightforward criticism of her newfound attraction. So, directly, we see a theme of opposites attracting not only through the relationship but also the words being used. We will see that a primary theme of the poem is "illusion," though "allusion" is extremely important to this poem. There are probably as many allusions as there are illusions (dozens) happening in the poem, and this complexity will offer us an extraordinarily layered reading.

The second stanza lets us know what she's reading. Instead of Foucault, that famous literary atheist, she happens to be enjoying Saint Ignatius, a fifteenth century father of the faith. The speaker of the poem responds to her through us by letting us know what he thinks of this. "Naivete / Aroused her, so she guided me to Chartres / And Sacre Coeur."

We understand that the poem takes place in Paris, the city of love. It shouldn't surprise us that at the traditional volta, or turn, between the octave and sestet, the lovers go from Paris to Rome, from the City of Love to the Eternal City. This is a journey that Robert Lowell famously makes (in the opposite direction) in the first poem of his well-known collection *Life Studies,* as he begins turning away from an intense period of Catholic faith. In Brock's poem, the parenthetical is simple yet profound: "for Paris hadn't been enough." Erotic love is never enough because it is imperfect, mortal, and (as C.S. Lewis shows in his book *The Four Loves*) based in "need-love"; whereas the love of God is all gift and immortal. Despite being in the Holy City, these two lovers don't hold back their carnal love, having relations on the wooden floor and then continuing their travels as lovers of art; they try to allow both loves to exist in harmony. And as anyone who might have ever watched The Dating Game or The Bachelor or any popular romantic comedy, we're hooked. Remember that in the theater a comedy is a play that ends with a wedding. We want to know what happens next. Will they end up together happily ever after? There's not much room in the sonnet, so we know it won't take long before we find out.

We have begun to see that not only the rhyme words offer opposition, but other polarities/binaries have appeared: Foucault and Ignatius, naivete and knowledge, passion and Passion (human and Divine), Paris and Rome (the city of love and the city of God), eros and agape, pilgrim and pagan, floor and ceiling, flatness and three-dimensionality, male and female, the true and the false, lover and beloved, faith and doubt. All this in one sonnet, and deftly done. For instance, Brock might have had the lovers having relations anywhere, but he chooses the "worn parquet." The floor is very subtly placed in opposition to the ceiling that we'll later encounter. And the painting on that ceiling is one of a heavenly rapture rather than an earthly one. The poet here is using every detail of the poem to reinforce this struggle of bringing opposites together. We might be reminded of Genesis 2:18: "It is not good that man should be alone."

However, from the beginning we might have suspected the relationship was too good to be true. Is a fall (and not just falling in love) coming? Notice the simile in the first line: "like lovers in movies." We know that Hollywood is not real: riding off into the sunset, happily ever after…. Sure, the hopeless romantics among us want to believe it, and we spend billions of dollars going to the movies (or these days having them come to us through our streaming services and satellite dishes). Indeed, for Brock, hope is the final concept in the poem. Hope and doubt. I would argue that it's not just a hope of romantic love but one of divine love. Brock writes "a hoped-for depth." The famous scripture from Hebrews, offering a profound definition of faith, calls it "the substance of things *hoped for*, the evidence of things not seen" (emphasis mine).

What have we seen? Sadly, an illusion. But a beautiful illusion. If you have ever been to Rome, to the church called Sant'Ignazio, you will have witnessed one of the greatest tromp l'oeil (trick of the eye) paintings in the world. Andrea Pozzo's canvas covers a portion of the ceiling toward the center of the church, the *transept* or the crossing. If you stand on a disk specifically placed below and before the painting and look up toward the altar, you will witness an extraordinary illusion. From that vantage point, you believe that this painting on the ceiling of the church is a monstrous dome, when in fact it is completely flat. Move off that disk ten feet, and the illusion disappears; you begin to see how the figures and curvature of the painting are all elongated to work from only that singular position and perspective. And isn't that the way of erotic love? The fantasy of Hollywood: "You complete me," Tom Cruise famously says to Renee Zellwegger. Or love at first sight, we might call it—the illusion of complete fulfillment in another from one important perspective and moment of the relationship. One need only move slightly off the mark to begin to notice the failures and peccadillos and perhaps even physical flaws. "Distance makes the heart grow fonder," someone said. Someone else said, "Distance makes the heart go wander." Which will it be?

The two characters in Brock's poem are not married, and therefore the sexual love they engage in is contrary to Judeo-Christian strictures. The pilgrim here is not perfect, and we don't know much detail about her story. The point of view in the poem is via the pagan. A beautiful contrary to her sin is the pagan's spiritual education, finally his going to church, albeit to see artifice and art, but open to spiritual transformation. Unfortunately, the search for spiritual truth is shut down by the end of the poem. Or is it?

First, we know via dramatic irony that the dome is an illusion. Second, despite the hoped-for depth and the swearing that he finally sees a dome (his eyes have been opened), we realize the poem here is in the past tense. He "swore" he saw the three-dimensional architecture. The swearing as an oath could be seen as a kind of pious gesture at first. But no, ultimately, after all that we have learned, the swear might seem a curse. The Book of James reiterates what Jesus had instructed, warning against swearing: to "Let your Yea be yea, and your Nay nay." And there the poem ends, the long O of the word dome ringing empty in our ears. I ask students whether they imagine that the two are still together by the end of the poem, and there seems to be always a healthy disagreement cut right down the middle.

But I believe the poem ends without any hope for romantic or divine love in relation to these two. The whole relationship seems to end in one big deception and, if so, is heartbreaking.

***

While Pozzo's painting in Sant'Ignazio is the great work of art people come to see, there is yet more illusion present in the church, and it acts as another kind of opposite. The fresco across the nave ceiling depicts St. Ignatius welcomed into heaven by Mary and Jesus. Here we have the opposite effect of the dome painting where the flat surface appears to be curved. If one stands upon a different disk at the entrance of the church, the curve of the nave ceiling appears as if it were made of straight columns ascending toward heaven. Here we have one more illusion of opposites. One last illusion to mention: Andrea Pozzo's canvas painting of the dome was destroyed in 1891, so the painting one sees now is a reproduction. All this illusion, and one both loses faith yet also can participate in the beauty of art.

What is artifice good for? Why do we enjoy being fooled in just the right way? We can't get enough of a great illusion or magic trick. Most of us love being fooled in one way or another. We want to believe someone can escape, pull a rabbit out of a hat, or even cheat death. Yet we know death is the one certainty. Ultimately, there must be some sort of fascinating trick of the eye to escape the law of life and death. We want to be fooled, and yet we don't want to be a fool. We want to know how the trick works, and we look for the sleight of hand.

One of the most famous and misread American poems is Robert Frost's "The Road not Taken." Many people refer to it as "The Road Less Traveled." As a matter of fact, many people convince themselves that the point of the poem (there is never only one point to a poem, so this is yet one more failure) is that the "road less traveled by" is the better road. Frost never says that. Read it for yourself. The poem is ultimately praising human choice. The ability and freedom to choose is more beautiful and wonderful and mysterious than the choice itself. To appreciate that, one has to be willing to be vulnerable and in a state of unknowing, or at least not all-knowing. The first sin was one of pride: the determination to know absolutely, without vulnerability or dependence on the Creator. The first illusion is for Satan to proclaim that "you both shall be like gods, knowing good and evil." According to the creation story in Genesis 1:26, they *already* were like God (rather than gods). "Let us make man in our image," the Word says. They knew the difference between right and wrong. Satan is like a modern-day advertiser. He robs you of your self-esteem, and then he sells it back to you at the price of the product.

Like Frost's famous crossroads poem, Geoffrey Brock's poem "Exercitia Spiritualia" displays for us an extraordinarily rendered and polarized world. It argues that, despite this bifurcation of the world in which we live, if we only have some faith, we can be complete. But even so, sometimes we have faith in things that are not real, and that illusion cannot satisfy. Faith, however, is not devoid of reason, and might just be a more humble knowledge that recognizes its limitations. I would argue, on this basis, that Brock's poem is a poem of faith.

A good poem always, by the end, throws us back up into the poem wanting and looking for more. If I allow myself to be taken all the way back to the title, I ask what exactly are these "spiritual exercises" developed by Ignatius. They are a series of meditations to be done over a period of a month connecting the believer, through Jesus, to God. They are to be done in solitude, and yet a part of the process involves submitting oneself to a spiritual authority or guide who helps one move through the exercises. When we consider this aspect of the poem, we might come to understand that, while we may have need of a guide in learning and love and life, we ultimately need solitude too. We must make up our own minds, walking alone toward the final vision of what is the purpose of our love and our lives, which we must not believe is some mere beautiful illusion.

Who's The Boss:
Victoria Chang's "I Once Was a Child"

I Once Was a Child

I once was a child am a child am someone's child
    not my mother's not my father's the boss
gave us special treatment treatment for something
        special a lollipop or a sticker glitter from the

toy box the better we did the better the plastic prize made
    in China one year everyone got a spinning top
one year everyone got a tap on their shoulders
        one year everyone was fired everyone

fired but me one year we all lost our words one year
    my father lost his words to a stroke
a stroke of bad luck stuck his words
        used to be so worldly his words fired

him let him go without notice can they do that
    can she do that yes she can in this land she can
once we sang songs around a piano *this land is your land*
        this land is my land in this land someone always

owns the land in this land someone who owns
    the land owns the buildings on the land owns
the people in the buildings unless an earthquake
        sucks the land in like a long noodle

***

A few years back I served my second stint as director of the creative writing program at Texas Tech University where I have taught for twenty years. I announced this on social media, and the news was met with great congratulations: thumbs up emojis, hearts, "wows," and many exclamation points. I didn't intend to announce this as any kind of achievement, only as news for professional reasons: mainly, so that if anybody wanted to work with us or study in our program, they would know that I was now the new point person. Anyone who has ever directed a creative writing program knows that this position is a gigantic time suck and there is very little to celebrate, unless you like administrative work. Very few writers I know like administrative work. There are dozens of fires to put out every semester including both faculty and student complaints, occasionally in the very sketchy areas of sexual harassment or discrimination, which anyone in their right mind wants to avoid like the plague. But somebody needs to take the reins of a program, and every once in a while you take one for the team.

Mostly the job requires juggling all the teaching schedules, recruiting, coordinating with the other programs in the department, dealing with curriculum changes and assessments, setting up meetings, organizing graduate applications, and other mind-numbing things that creative people don't normally like to do. Also, wannabe writers from outside the university sometimes call, wanting to know how they might get published. Yes, just a few years ago I actually had an office phone that plugged into the wall, and people would call me.

The congratulations heaped upon me by my friends was mostly by those who had never done this kind of thing before. I think, in some ways, people saw me as "the boss." But there was no pay raise. There was a course reduction, so I taught fewer classes. From the outside, for any of my friends teaching four or five courses per semester, my reduced two-course per semester load at a research university looked pretty good. However, this kind of administrative work can be more time-consuming than teaching classes. And I didn't get to boss anyone around about anything. I was more like the oldest child in a family who, due only to seniority, is saddled with the most duties and expectations, which includes taking out the trash. I'm not complaining, though. When I was in college, I worked for four years on a loading dock just south of Atlanta moving freight in and out of tractor trailers all night long. I know what work is.

Creative writing programs are often housed within English depart-
ments. In most English departments these days, there is a great attraction
to theory, especially French philosophical/linguistic literary theory that is
fairly impenetrable and uninteresting, if not absolutely boring, to any un-
dergraduate student. Many, if not most, English professors approach the
literature of their specialized areas (18th century fiction, Modern British,
Asian-American literature, etc.) through a theoretical way of reading texts
rather than through the love of them as art works. On the other hand, most
undergraduates who read books have done so most of their lives because of
beauty, because they love being lost (and found) in the story of a novel or
the song of a poem. This older approach, the love of literature, or philology,
comes from *philo* (love) of *logos* (words). Clearly then, there is a divide be-
tween these approaches to the literary text and how it is meant to be read.
It's a good question: what is literature for?

These days, the idea of philology is understood as old-fashioned, and
sometimes laughed at. Not by me. I have a kind of "ubi sunt" response to
philology: O, for those good old days when people used to love words,
music, and story for their own sakes. Well, it's not that simple, and I'm not
that simple either. But a lot of the excitement of the craft of writing that
used to be at the heart of English departments has been pushed away from
the literature courses (reading) over to only the creative writing programs
(writing). And even many of these writing programs have become intoxi-
cated by theory and politics. When I say *love*, I don't mean my passionate
swooning and leaning against a wall with a book in my hand, or standing
on top of a desk with my hand on my chest spouting passages from Percy
Bysshe Shelley. I just mean that I find this combination of metaphors, of
this rhyme, or that allusion to be so pregnant with meaning that I then see
the world, as Elizabeth Bishop suggested, through the lens of this poem for
the next twenty-four hours. But I do love it. And I can show students how
a great metaphor works or why a certain rhyme matters to a final couplet.
I see a poem as Donald Hall sees it, as a "language machine," and I like to
get under the hood as well as drive the car.

One of my problems with contemporary theory is that it can give us
too narrow a lens by which to view the work. Recently, literature theorists

have fallen in love with the word *lens*. You can't understand a work unless you see it through the right lens, they claim. A lens of disability, a lens of trauma, a lens of ecofeminism… But the idea of a lens suggests that there is a correct and ideal way of seeing, not that we have to shift gears for each and every type of literature we come across.

While I find many of these literary theories valuable and interesting, in and of themselves they seem less powerful to me than looking at the aesthetic and formal framework of the poem at hand. Feminist theory recognizes how the text bears witness to the patriarchal oppression and inequality of women in society. A reader can apply a feminist critique to Homer's *Odyssey* to show how Odysseus is not held to the same standard of marital fidelity as Penelope. One could argue that the entire story revolves around a wife's central role in the home. Clytemnestra, Helen, Arete and Penelope are all on display as either positive or negative examples. Men are held to no such standard.

Another popular theoretical framework, deconstruction, takes a typical reading of a work of art and turns it on its head; it tries to undermine received knowledge about a given literary work and see the work anew, often by making an opposite claim. We might take Atticus Finch in *To Kill a Mockingbird* and show how he is not actually a character of great compassion and forward thinking about race, but one who is in many ways a racist continuing the oppression of people of color.

Another, psychoanalytic theory, views a text in the way that Freud might have: looking for its psychosexual connotations and exploring the difficult familial conflicts tied up in a poem or story. A reader might explore Robert Lowell's poems in *Life Studies* to understand how the poet's Freudian obsessions with his father and mother color the poems, even the ones that don't seem to be concerned with family. For instance, the poems "For George Santayana" or "Skunk Hour" examine the various characters and speakers, or even the poet himself, psychoanalyzing them concerning trauma, sexuality, family and so on.

Most theories revolve around the idea that there are certain power dynamics at play within the work and associated with the cultures, characters, and authors involved. Then with this view to the work, theorists make a critique of the social order then and now. That critique always involves someone or some groups being treated unfairly. While this is no doubt valuable for understanding the literature at hand, as well as the world around us, often the view of the beautiful way the story is told or how the poem is sung can become unimportant or altogether lost. I have recently heard theoretical arguments that suggest aesthetics (simply, the theory of beauty) actually gets in the way of social critique, that studying beauty can be in and of itself harmful.

At its best, theory can help us come to terms with our social order through literature and understand how to become better people who pursue and understand more deeply social justice and the environment. One semester, in my sophomore introduction to poetry course, among many other things we discussed the poems of Plath and Homer in relation to the sexual misconduct news that we hear about every day. The connections are obvious, even reaching to the highest office of the President of the United States. There is no doubt that literature from antiquity to present addresses head-on the violence perpetrated on our most vulnerable. But my aim in this course is to discuss the beauty of poetry, and how poems address sexual issues is only one small part of what a poem does if it does that at all.

At its worst, however, theory ends up dwelling on the failings of the author, the texts, or the world around us, tattling on the poem or story or society for its bad behavior according to the current worldview. It can lead to a kind of false sense of superiority ("Look how racist those other people were") or even schadenfreude ("I feel pretty good once I see how others suffer"). Sometimes, the critic or scholar may end up merely subverting the text for the sake of subverting the social order.

This technique is valuable to some professors; a kind of religion made of tearing down institutions and canons. In some perverse way, the reader/critic becomes intellectually superior to the writer (which is hardly ever true of any young student of literature), and not even the best works can stand up to someone bent on "subverting" or undermining them for the sake of pulling down authority—at least not when that is the only measure of the text. Anyway, the authors are not there to defend themselves, nor do they often have advocates present. Marxism, which offers another theoretical way of reading, suggests that the natural order of our lives involves social antagonisms between economic classes which ultimately result in the upper classes oppressing the lower and finally the lower tearing down the upper. So if we can see that a literary work is elitist in any way, we can and should tear it or aspects of it down. Some build sandcastles, and some come along and knock them down. Both actions bring pleasure. But we might ask ourselves which is the more creative act?

Here in the 21st century, human rights are more codified and recognized than ever. With these human rights comes power to the individual and limits on authority. Civil disobedience is permitted, even championed. Ultimate authorities are checked and balanced, hopefully, to allow individuals freedom and mobility. Yet mere anarchy is a threat to the individual. Everyone needs protection at one time or another. We must constantly negotiate how authorities both defend and exploit us.

When it comes to reading poetry, perhaps it might be valuable to think about how believers approach scripture. When we open up the Bible, those of us who have embraced the gospel hope that the Holy Spirit will make that mind in us unified with the one who wrote it (and the God who inspired the writer) rather than coming to the verses with itching ears, wanting it to tell us what we want to hear. A poor reader wants it to be more like a photoshopped selfie—only our best aspects reflected in its pages—rather than a lamp that might show our defects as well as our good traits. So then, to what degree should a student or scholar of literature cultivate humility before a text? To what degree might we approach the work of art with a little humility rather than looking to satisfy our own ends? Sure, it is a false comparison, because no one thinks that an author's poem or novel is inerrant, as some think of scripture. But a little respect for the author as a creator of beauty might go a long way.

***

I have come here to praise Victoria Chang, not to bury her in the worst aspects of academia, its theoretical undermining of the beauty of poems. But, first, she has a book of poems called *The Boss*, and second, I aim to make my introduction to this chapter relevant in several ways. I hope to give her the praise due her genius, trying to draw more readers to her work, especially by trying to get at the importance of authority all around us. So now, if you will, go back to the beginning of the chapter, and re-read this beautiful poem.

Her poem "I Once Was a Child" is the first poem in her collection, *The Boss*. All of the poems in this book revolve around the idea of an employee dealing with her boss, or the various bosses of her work and professional life, as well as being the boss in various aspects of her personal life. My long preamble to this essay aims to help us understand that power structures are of great interest to all of us. We fight against them for righteous reasons, but we also partake in them for self-preservation. Power structures don't exist on their own without beauty permeating every aspect of our lives.

The word *boss* carries widely different connotations. A boss can be seen as someone who looks out for you and runs an operation smoothly, but also she/he can be considered the one who keeps you down and makes your life miserable. Some of my poetry students affectionately call me "Boss," but is it affection? And for a while, maybe it was the '80s, people complimented something cool by calling it "boss." If they like something, often my kids will say it's "lit." I like to pretend that's short for "literature."

Intelligently, and with obvious design, "I Once Was a Child" begins at or near the beginning in a multiplicity of ways. First, we are obviously at the beginning of the book. As well, the word "Once" conjures up the phrase "Once upon a time," so you consider that you might be at the start of a longer narrative. The word in the title and thrice in the first line, "child," obviously indicates a beginning stage of life and an open-eyed perspective. It puts us at ease in this way. In this first line we move from past to present quickly through the "was...am" construction: "was a child am a child am someone's child." We also get a frenetic pacing to the language, perhaps a child's excited stammering through a sentence unhindered by any punctuation.

Before too long, we will realize that the poem has no punctuation at all. This is a harder feat than you would imagine. While people in ancient times were able to write without punctuation, we are now highly dependent upon it for clarity and precision. Many novice poets think it's cool or interesting to do away with punctuation, but they mostly fail. There are only a few poets I know who can do without it and make the lack of punctuation work for them in a positive way.

Victoria Chang is among these few. The way to do it is to understand the problems that arise when you *don't* use punctuation. And the primary problem that a poet will face is unintentionally creating for readers ungrammatical or awkward ambiguities. Since we don't quite know, according to commas and periods, where phrases and sentences stop, we have to depend upon the writer to make it absolutely clear through other means. We don't want to apply the subject to the wrong predicate and the predicate to the wrong object, and so on. The words must be arranged just so, in order that we intuitively begin to recognize where to pause, even within the lines. We know that we can pause at the ends of the lines, as the white space there definitely acts as a kind of delay, even as a complete stop sometimes. But beyond that, in a poem without punctuation there will be a lot of guesswork for a reader in figuring out how the grammar works.

The speaker of Chang's poem makes us realize the power dynamic of the workplace can seem like a family dynamic where the authorities are not only in charge, but they treat us like children. The incentives we get sometimes from work are a joke, and it pleases us to realize these trifles are not why we do a good job. Here "the plastic prize made / in China" is important not only because it relates to us that this is a bauble of little value or cheap manufacture, but that it is from China, the place of the author's ancestry. While we cannot assume that the poem is strictly biographical (the speaker could be an invention of the poet's imagination), biography still might aid us in understanding the poem and complicating its perspective. Chang is a Chinese name. Victoria Chang, the author of this poem, is the daughter of Taiwanese immigrants, so this adds an odd tension to the poem.

But geography and biography aside, we know that things made in China are culturally problematic because they often signify for us Americans something less valuable or even done at the expense of child labor. From the assorted cheap prizes, to the ambiguous tap on the shoulder (it could mean you're doing a good job, like a pat on the back, or it might mean "get back to work"), to the notice of firings, the office seems like a difficult place to be. Another biographical note: Victoria Chang has made her living differently than most of us poets who make our actual living by teaching. Rather than working as a professor, until recently she had a business career in marketing and communications. In his popular book *Can Poetry Matter?*, published back in 1991, poet and critic Dana Gioia suggested that perhaps one of the reasons for contemporary poetry's obscurity was due to the fact that poetry had become too insular, too isolated in academia, and we needed poets who had regular every day jobs as did poets like William Carlos Williams, Wallace Stevens, and Weldon

Kees. Regardless, we are likely to have bosses hanging over us, providing us some of the pressure and suffering we need to write good poems. For instance, I have to answer to my chair, my dean, and ultimately the state of Texas. And Texas is a boss like no other.

Notice that these opening lines in Chang's poem set us in opposition to the boss, encouraging us to oppose this authority. Then, when everyone else in the office is fired, the speaker of the poem is isolated. At this point, the poem shifts. The losses and failures extend beyond the office. Words are lost. For a poet, this is the greatest failure. Her father "lost his words to a stroke / a stroke of bad luck stuck his words." There are multiple ironies here. While we come to the understanding that the father's health has failed, and the resulting condition is one of wordlessness, the poet begins to play with the language. This could seem insensitive, but I see it as a triumphant and courageous maneuver.

The poet won't settle for no words. The poet realizes that she has enough words for her and her father and through the play of language (remember, she "once was a child"), she can get deeply at some things a more straightforward and "serious" poem couldn't. Notice how the play with the sound of the words advances from "words" to "stroke" twice, to "luck" to "stuck," back to "words" to "worldly," and yet again to "words." Also, "stuck" seems like it might be "struck," because "stuck" is not a transitive verb. The grammar gets sticky here, as we pick our way through it.

Her word play doesn't end here. She notes that her father's "words fired him." She has witnessed her colleagues fired with words, but her own father is fired *by* words, or his loss of them. Words are the ultimate boss here. They are *the* authority. In his extraordinary and famous autobiography, Frederick Douglass discusses his learning the ABCs and how this very action of mastering words, though he was a slave, became the first step in his freedom from slavery. This is true for all of us in relation to language; literacy is empowering. If the poet can control language and beautifully contain its form, she can perhaps find some power over this very difficult situation in which she feels powerless, both at work and with family. In other poems later in the book, Chang's speaker has a young daughter who really shows who's boss. This family dynamic throughout investigates the extraordinarily complex power structures involved with being a daughter, an employee, a boss, a mother, and a poet. But words are difficult and not always so easily mastered, especially for the very young or the very old. They can "let you go without notice."

The poem moves forward with questions (without question marks): "can they do that / can she do that." Notice that the words are both "they" and "she." One might think of the poetic muse, which is usually figured as female. But at this point, we could be shifting back to the earlier conversation about the boss, who in this poem is female. The poem also shifts back to the subtle conversation about nationality and place, patriotically declaring that "she can in this land she can." In America, the free market economy might be free, but you are always, also, free to be fired.

The poet playfully toys with Woody Guthrie's famous folk song as she reflects back to some childhood memory of presumably her family singing around a piano, "this land is your land / this land is my land," which pairs very well with the way Chang has been using repetition in her own style throughout the poem. At this moment, one realizes that her immigrant parents might have a deep desire to embrace the romantic American dream, as fraught with faulty power dynamics as it may be, especially to someone of a different race in an earlier time. It takes courage and a kind of faith to believe in the dream. But it seems the speaker of the poem becomes a little bitter or ironic when she says that "someone always // owns the land." And whoever owns the land (not the employee) owns the building and even "owns / the people," though ultimately all is owned by something bigger because at any moment tragedy, such as an act of God, could strike: "an earthquake / sucks the land in like a long noodle." That's the end of the poem, with no period. We end on the word "noodle" which is definitely a silly word in comparison with all the dark aspects of this poem: firings, a stroke, the failure of language, an earthquake. And then a noodle?

I believe that the poet is not only being playful with this image, but serious too. Seeing the land sucked in like a long noodle is seeing it from a God's eye view. Ultimately, we do come to the perspective that though people and money and bosses and parents and ourselves sometimes are in charge, there is something beyond us acting as "the boss." Is it just nature? That's a possibility for this poem, no doubt. Chang doesn't explore this overtly, but I would argue she suggests this with great restraint. If we return to the first line, we remember that she suggests she is "someone's child." This reminds me of Elizabeth Bishop's poem "Filling Station" where she says at the end, "Somebody loves us all." That poem doesn't mention the mother in the poem at all, but so many of the details of the poem point to the maternal.

There is another recent and wonderful book with a boss obsession: Maurice Manning's book *Bucolics*. It is a series of poems addressed to someone named "Boss" who seems to be a farm supervisor. After reading for only a few stanzas, you realize that this boss is THE Boss, God, who is the Almighty. He runs the show because he created the show and everything in it. He is a trickster, a rewarder, and oftentimes incomprehensible, as his station seems so far removed from the voice of the poem who is just a common worker. Yet he seems as familiar as someone you work for who signs your paychecks. He seems benevolent, yet a man to be feared. The more Manning's farmhand humbles himself before this boss, it seems the more he discovers.

Victoria Chang's boss poems are very different than Manning's, though they both are enamored with this idea and problem of power, especially the authorial power of the word that lurks beneath the concept of labor, originally (See the Book of Genesis) understood as a curse. Chang, as author of these poems carries an extraordinary poise through her playfulness and in this lack of punctuation I noted earlier. Chang is so subtle in her use of words that a reader never feels she is bossy at all. She seems like a child at play, a precocious and witty child. And yet, she is a child who is clearly the boss, and simultaneously critical of her bosses.

***

Every parent knows the difficulty and the necessity of authority. As authors and creators of our children, we hopefully exercise power in order to protect these delicate ones rather than to only please ourselves. We act strongly and courageously, but also we realize the necessity for gentleness and humility in the exercise of our powers. We cede some of our authority to those under us to encourage individuality and fortitude, independence and creativity.

The same thing goes for poets in their relation to words, I think. One can boldly brandish a mastery of words, but if one doesn't show restraint, the work becomes either impenetrable or facile. A poet leaves certain ambiguities in a poem so that the reader can enter in and become, in some important way, a co-creator. If one is a believer in God, one recognizes the absolute majesty and almighty power of a Creator who can make a world from nothing. Every time I am faced with the grandeur of a view from a mountaintop, the onslaught of a coming West Texas storm, or the vast expanse of the ocean, I recognize authority as something not to be trifled with. I think of God finally making his appearance by showing his creative power to Job. Nature is not often something to be subverted. Yes, people climb Mount Everest, and those who succeed feel a great sense of achievement. Many die.

While earthly institutions are imperfect and limited, in many ways we know that we should cherish and even desire authority. Who doesn't recognize the beauty, comfort, and good afforded in the protection of a father or mother? As a parent, who doesn't feel the greatest sense of reward in having birthed, protected, and raised children with a guiding hand? In the church, the authority of a pastor is necessary for guidance and order, though this power is not without checks and balances. And a good pastor or a parent never lords it over those under their charge; if they are effective at what they do, they most often serve selflessly.

As for poets and novelists, well, I would argue that a grand respect for their authority goes a long way in appreciating what is happening on the page. That is not to say we can't be critical of how authority works and sometimes fails. I agree with literary theorists that we co-author any book we read because we bring to it our own imaginative use of words. And if there is an ideal and perfect Father in heaven above who has in mind our complete adoption with full rights to an eternal inheritance…what of that authority?

In the Lord's Prayer, the way Jesus teaches us to pray, He mentions one noun twice—the word *kingdom*. The prayer is very concise, so if something is repeated, we should take note. This word comes at the beginning and end of the prayer, as if to frame it, as if to let us know that we ought to know the big context: to Whom we are praying—a Father who is King. A king has full authority we refer to as sovereignty. Americans don't quite understand this experientially since we live under a representative government. A U.S. senator might have power, but he is not a king. What a king says goes. There are no checks and balances with God, especially with the King of heaven (that word is repeated twice), and this is a good thing because

His rule is without flaw. And it is strangely wonderful that He wants to make us His heirs.

When reading the Holy Scriptures, we believers not only have the church fathers and the original writers to thank as authors of this life-giving and life-affirming text, but we recognize the authority of the Spirit who guided them. This is the Boss who doesn't ultimately want to fire us but to, as the scriptures say, give us good things, make us in His image and, in a powerful way, promote us, making us the boss of our own realm. It is a privilege to co-exist in this dominion and sing with a voice of calm assurance "this land is your land, this land is my land" while believing that the land extends far beyond our wildest imagination to another realm where we find our names written, indeed, in a deed we call the Lamb's Book of Life.

Birds of a Feather:
George Herbert's "Easter-wings"

1.

Easter-wings.

LOrd, who createdst man in wealth and store,
    Though foolishly he lost the same,
      Decaying more and more,
        Till he became
          Most poore: *5*
          With   thee
        O let me rise
      As larks, harmoniously,
    And sing this day thy victories:
Then shall the fall further the flight in me.   *10*

My tender age in sorrow did beginne:
    And still with sicknesses and shame
      Thou didst so punish sinne,
        That I became
          Most thinne.   *15*
          With   thee
        Let me combine
      And feel this day thy victorie:
    For, if I imp my wing on thine,
Affliction shall advance the flight in me.   *20*

We have small Merlin falcons here in Lubbock, Texas. When one comes racing across the tops of the trees in my neighborhood, the smaller birds such as doves and sparrows scatter like an explosion and long silences follow.

Occasionally much larger Peregrines will hunt from one of the twelve-story dorms near the Texas Tech University English building. I have watched hundreds of pigeons wheeling around while a Peregrine toys with them, diving here and there, deciding which it will have for lunch. It is majestic and terrifying. Sometimes, before class, I have stood in the courtyard watching this otherworldly display while dozens of students walk by with their heads turned down at the electronic screens of their devices. I'm sure if they noticed me, they would think me strange for looking up. I feel bad for them watching their phones rather than what I witness above us in the outstretched wings of birds, displaying the power of life and death, approaching poetry.

This chapter is a little different than the others in this book in that it is more thoroughly scholarly, referencing literary scholars, formal concepts, and manuscript research. An earlier version of the essay appeared as a scholarly article in *Christianity & Literature*, and it took me several years to complete, revising it between teaching and other projects. I am a poet, and I usually leave this kind of critical work to others, but I kept discovering more and more information on Herbert's poem, and I had to keep digging. I wanted to include the essay without too many changes to show a very close look at one of the most beautiful poems ever written in English, and to discuss one way in which it may have been misread for nearly 400 years.

***

George Herbert was born in Wales in the late 16th century. An Anglican priest, he died from tuberculosis when he was only 39. Next to John Donne, he is now the most admired of the group of Renaissance writers we refer to as the Metaphysical poets. He is recognized as one of the greatest Christian lyric poets in the English language, though his poems were not published during his lifetime. Other than poetry, he is famous for his prose book of pastoral instruction, *A Priest to the Temple*, which claims at its outset "to set down the Form and Character of a true Pastour, that I may have a Mark to aim at."

He is also known for writing or translating from the French, Spanish and Italian nearly 1200 aphorisms called "Outlandish Proverbs" which you can find in his *Collected Works*. Many of them, such as these, are quite familiar:

- Man proposeth. God disposeth.
- When a friend askes, there is no to morrow.
- A child correct behind and not before
- Thinke of ease, but worke on.
- Advise none to marry or to goe to warre.
- Prayers and provender hinder no journey.
- Living well is the best revenge.
- Prayer should be the key of the day and the lock of the night.
- Helpe thy selfe, and God will helpe thee.
- The shortest answer is doing.
- The best mirror is an old friend.
- Good workemen are seldom rich.

But George Herbert is known most thoroughly as a poet. Many scholars would agree that his most famous poem is "Easter-wings." The fame of this poem is owed not only to the extraordinary meanings crafted throughout the poem, but also its very interesting form and shape: the words of the poem are arranged to create the shape of wings. It may very well be the most recognized "shape poem" in English. This visual pattern of the poem affects our understanding of the words and lines. How and why Herbert literally shaped this poem remains deeply important to our perception and enjoyment of it, though this *how* and *why* may have been completely misunderstood for a long time due to the way it was first, and is usually, printed: stanzas centered on the page in a couple shapes approximating hourglasses.

Some scholars, notably Randall McLeod, consider "Easter-wings" to be two individual poems rather than two stanzas. In this chapter, I'll consider it as one poem, as has nearly always been presented in print and referred to in criticism, though we ultimately must reckon with McLeod's reading of the poems.

To begin this chapter, instead of typing out my own version (as with the other poems in this book), I have given you an image of "Easter-wings" from *The Works of George Herbert* published by Oxford University Press in 1914. This presentation of the poem is close to how we usually see it, though sometimes modern spellings are used or the spacing is slightly altered. Later in the chapter (Image 2), you can see the earliest version of the printed poem that presented it sideways on the page. No matter how it has been presented or re-printed, "Easter-wings" is not easy reading.

In *The Poetry of George Herbert*, Helen Vendler complains that many earlier critical efforts to read Herbert's poems had their faults but could "be seen as a cooperative venture in learning to read him with greater attention." She notes that though Herbert had often been read superficially as a minor poet whose work remains in the shadow of John Donne's superior verse, "Herbert's apparent simplicity is deceptive." She discerns that critics had discussed "relatively few poems in aesthetic as well as moral terms," failing in "comprehensiveness of description" (Vendler 3). So it is ironic that even Vendler gives short shrift to Herbert's poem "Easter-wings," lending it only a cursory mention in her book, calling the first stanza "extremely conventional" rather than considering it in the aesthetic and moral terms she calls for (Vendler 145). However, if we consider the relationships that Herbert weaves among the poem's shape, its context, its allusions, and the effects of its formal structures, there seems little conventional about it.

Published some fifteen years after Vendler's book, Janis Lull's *The Poem in Time: Reading George Herbert's Revisions of The Church*, takes a closer look at the formal, literary, and textual choices that Herbert made in constructing his poems, and notably "Easter-wings." In her chapter "The Shape of Time," Lull states that Herbert's poems dealing with time

> are forms whose beginnings in one way or another "touch their End" (*Paradise*). Chiastic form makes readers experience the flow of time not as a line or a circle but as a symmetrical narrowing and widening process that finally returns to its beginnings in timeless truth. The revised Easter-wings makes the most obvious use of this chiastic form because each stanza appears as a visual X. (Lull 75)

Chiasmus, a rhetorical figure or literary device in which words or concepts are repeated in reverse order, makes a mirroring of the repeated words or phrases. Christians understand that the creation of the world features a beginning in the garden of Paradise. Though the paradise of the Garden of Eden is in the scriptures soon lost, there remains a hope for a reversal: the ultimate return to a restored Paradise, a reunion of a perfect relationship with God. This is a type of narrative chiasmus, and the Bible is rife with chiastic structures such as this to illustrate the idea of redemption or renewal. "Easter-wings" displays both narrative and structural chiasmus; it begins with "wealth and store." Though this gift is "lost" (as the lines get thinner), the first stanza ends with restoration toward a "rise" and then "flight" (as the lines lengthen back out). The second stanza moves from the speaker's "tender" beginnings to "sorrow," "sicknesses," "sinne," and "shame" only to rebound toward "victorie" and "flight."

The shape of "Easter-wings" offers the reader more than just chiasmus. Robert Halli claims that the image of the stanzas in the Bodleian manuscript (Image 4) of "Easter-wings" make a "triple hieroglyph" of crosses, wings, and hourglasses. One can see how each of these suggested images communicates theologically complex principles. The cross on which these stanzas (the shape defined by the white space along the edges of the words, an *x* rather than a *t*— St. Andrew's Cross) are hung represents the crux of the story of Jesus (indeed, the very crossroads of time according to our calendar) and the individual speaker's personal story of salvation. The wings complement the lark and the suggested falcon of the poem, and emphasize flight and a defiance of gravity. The image of the hourglass suggests the downward fall of its sand to measure time. Time running out is an image suggestive of death, though one might see the body of the sand altered from one life to another in a fullness and accretion below rather than just an emptiness above. Herbert's poem "Church Monuments" contains the wonderful idea of a tapering human form related to the hourglass: "That flesh is but the glasse, which holds the dust / That measures all our time; which also shall / Be crumbled into dust (20–22)"; here the hourglass is not the shape of the text but rather an image suggested to the mind's eye. In "Easter-wings," this visible shape of the text of the poem, of time, this *memento mori*, serves as a reminder of our time running out, our return to dust. Yet Christian theology professes that Jesus overcomes death on Easter and, like the famous Phoenix of mythology, rises on metaphorical wings from this dust of death. As the Apostles' Creed states, "On the third day he rose from the dead. / He ascended into heaven."

Later in the seventeenth century, John Dryden derided the kinds of graphic display we see in "Easter-wings" as something too easily achieved through the manipulation of type. In his poem, "Mac Flecknoe," mocking fellow poet Thomas Shadwell, he writes this couplet:

There thou may'st wings display and altars raise,
And torture one poor word ten thousand ways.

I agree with Dryden that shape poems generally make for notoriously bad poems. Why? Because the shape usually does only one thing: that is, the poem provides *one* textual image without doing the usual work that poems do, breaking the lines in meaningful places to create myriad effects. A good poem makes with language more than just one effect on every line as well as with nearly every image, sound, syntactical choice, allusion, and all the other literary devices it employs. Herbert's stanza form does all this, conjuring up a multiplicity of images (the X of a cross, wing, hourglass) within the visual shape of the word patterns. If the shape of these stanzas, these wings, represented only one verbal/visual display of wit, perhaps it might be a limited exercise (imagine any simple devotional poem jammed into the shape of a cross), but Herbert's shape offers us much more. With the recent development of computer and printer technologies, it is easier than ever for poets to arrange poems into interesting shapes that might seem meaningful. However, sadly, most of these poems offer only technological rather than literary manipulations. Often, a contemporary poem's centeredness is our first clue to its imaginative failure. These poems often rely too much on the image created by type rather than the images that might be invested in the words. On the contrary, in "Easter-wings" the movement of the eye, in and back out, twice, is meaningful through the complexity of its form and function.

Herbert's shapely form strengthens already strong lines. The belief that man is made in God's image, fallen, and then restored is at the heart of the formal logic here. The linear contraction and expansion create a form twice mirrored. Both top and bottom of the two stanzas create mirrored triangular forms. And the manuscript version of the poem, as well as its early printings, presents each stanza on a separate facing page, such that the shapes on the pages mirror or parallel each other. These formal patterns are essential to our understanding of the poem's content. The first stanza begins with a direct address to the "Lord" and ends with the word "me." There is a representation of humility in that progression, yet both persons are connected by the one long sentence of the stanza. The extended syntax creates a unity between the Lord and the speaker. The Lord creates "man" in the first and longest line "in wealth and store." The second line, shorter by a metrical foot, physically illustrates the loss of those riches, recalling to us the creation story in Genesis where Paradise is lost rather quickly. The second line features the word "lost," the third "decaying," and the fourth "Most poore." By the time we have arrived at the bottom of the funnel, man's life has diminished both literally (in the content) and figuratively (in the form). And the diminishment is not just visual but aural. There is one fewer prosodic foot in each line as we move down the page.

As soon as we have arrived at the stanza's point of greatest contraction, the expansion back out to fullness begins. Well, almost. The next line, "With thee," is actually the shortest line. Here, we cross over the center of the chiasmus, or the cross, its most intense yet rarefied moment. This line can indicate both the incarnation and the crucifixion. The "thee" in the phrase "With thee" recalls Immanuel, "God with us," who is laid below "Most poore" mankind. Both the baby Jesus and the crucified Christ are suggested in these words, but I tend to read them as primarily the latter due to the next line: "O let me rise." Most Christians would argue that we can be raised from death only by the power of the *resurrected* Christ—not by the birth alone. The rest of the stanza's expansion features the speaker rising as, appropriately, birds: "As larks, harmoniously" singing a song of praise of and from a *felix culpa*. Note that the poet rises in unison with Christ, in a plurality with Him, not merely as imitation after Him.

To add to the complexity of the visual movement, a harmony of rhymes audibly weaves the lines of each stanza together: ababacdcdc. The three *a* rhymes brace the two *b* rhymes, and the three *c* rhymes brace the two *d* rhymes in both halves of the stanza (each wing), holding the halves together sonically and visually. The poem's rhyme could be an extension of its meaning, reflecting the embrace of Christ around mankind and possibly suggesting that our story is interwoven with His. Indeed, though the "Man" in line 1 can be understood as Adam (and by extension, mankind in Paradise), this person could also be seen as the Incarnated Christ who loses all to become "Most poore." Jesus is "Most poore" in that he gives up his omnipotence/omnipresence to live as a person, but also "Most poore" in the way that he suffers and dies on the cross.

Though the *h* of "he" is not capitalized in the poem, Christ can be considered the subject, but ironically. The second line of the poem mentions that "foolishly he lost the same." Paul's first letter to the Corinthians states in its opening that "We preach Christ crucified, to the Jews a stumbling block and the Greeks foolishness, but to those who are called, both Jews and Greeks, Christ the power of God and the wisdom of God." The idea of the resurrection from the dead may have seemed foolish or impossible to the Greeks and Jews of his day, but Paul understands this doctrine to be the cornerstone of his theology. Later in the same letter, in I Corinthians 15, Paul writes: "And if Christ is not risen, then our preaching is empty and your faith is also empty...you are still in your sins." That we can read both the incarnation and crucifixion here into the same line—"Most poore"—is a fine ambiguity. Both are turning points in human history, one marking earthly Time and the other marking Spiritual Time, one marking the earthly birth of the God-man and the other the spiritual re-birth, "the firstborn among many brethren."

A similar pattern, both visual and thematic, develops in the next stanza, though we begin not as in the first stanza with the creation of man, but now with the speaker of the poem. The prior stanza ended with "me" and this following stanza begins "My tender age." This reversal enacts the Christian concept of the last becoming first. In this second stanza, we will have a more intimate picture of the fall—another beginning, but this time personal rather than abstract. Rather than "man," we have the speaker, the *I*, moving from "sorrow" to "sicknesses and shame," so we understand that he is confessing his "sinne." And we might infer that sin results in the speaker becoming "Most thinne." As in the prior stanza, we see that this is neither the "Most poore" or "Most thinne" line. The shortest line, again, is "With thee," once more indicating that though a person might grow poor or thin or feel afflicted, Jesus suffered more. Indeed, as Philippians 2:6–7 reports, Jesus emptied himself, becoming the least of men: "who, being in the form of God, did not consider it robbery to be equal with God, but made Himself of no reputation, taking the form of a bondservant, and coming in the likeness of men." The white space encroaching on the words at the center of the page visually demonstrates this notion of desolation. Moreover, in the tenth chapter of Mark, Jesus tells the rich young ruler: "sell whatever you have and give to the poor, and you will have treasure in heaven; and come, take up the cross, and follow Me." Jesus was asking this rich man to become "Most poore." Not only must one become poor to enter the kingdom of God, but one must take up one's own cross, becoming "Most thinne." Herbert could very well have this story in mind when arriving at the center of each stanza: "With thee." As in the previous stanza, right after this shortest line, the line lengths expand through the rest of the poem. To grow most thin with God is to be stretched out on our own crosses of sacrificial living and dying to self so that we ultimately might be renewed.

The form of the poem's verse is significant at the level of the line and the stanza, and also as it resolves into the shape of the entire poem. Originally, though posthumously, the poem "Easter-wings" was printed sideways on two pages, probably to show more clearly the formal design of outspread wings:

2.

34   *The Church.*

¶ Easter-wings,

Lord, who createdst man in wealth and store,
Though foolishly he lost the same,
Decaying more and more,
Till he became
Most poore:
With thee
O let me rise
As larks, harmoniously,
And sing this day thy victories:
Then shall the fall further the flight in me.

¶ Easter-

The Church.   35

¶ Easter-wings,

My tender age in sorrow did beginne:
And still with sicknesses and shame
Thou didst so punish sinne,
That I became
Most thinne.
With thee
Let me combine,
And feel this day thy victorie:
For, if I imp my wing on thine,
Affliction shall advance the flight in me.

¶ H. Ba-

A reader might assume that this layout was Herbert's wish, but no one can be sure. We don't have any of Herbert's instructions as to his desired look or shape of the poem. Only two early manuscript versions of the poem survive, and each one has a distinct and similar shape, though these shapes are unlike the first and subsequent print versions. These manuscripts were written by secretaries or copyists, probably directly from Herbert's versions. The two are sometimes called the Williams manuscript, otherwise known as W (from the Dr. Williams Library in London) and the Bodleian manuscript, otherwise known as B (in the Bodleian Library at Oxford). Here are the images of both W and B, respectively:

3.

Scholars have suggested that the Williams manuscript (next page, with authorial corrections) should be considered a work in progress from the early 1610s into the 1620s. Amy Charles's *The Williams Manuscript of George Herbert's Poems* establishes that it was written by a secretary, and the corrections were done in Herbert's own handwriting. This is important because the shape of it was, by virtue of Herbert's own handwriting, not corrected by him: since Herbert wrote corrections on this page, he at least acknowledged the shape without amending it. The more neat and lovely hand of the Bodleian manuscript was done by a Little Gidding calligrapher shortly after Herbert's death in 1633 under the direction of Herbert's close friend, Nicholas Ferrar (Cesare xix, xxii). In each manuscript version, the intended shape is neither left-justified (as in most of Herbert's other poems, with their standard indentations) nor centered.

4.

C.C. Brown and W.P. Ingoldsby notice some extraordinary aspects of the poem having to do with the shape and whence Herbert may have borrowed it. Specifically, they keenly identify some literary allusions, including one to a Greek poet, Simmias of Rhodes. Simmias had written (prior to 300 B.C.) a shape poem that looks remarkably like the first print version of "Easter-wings." This image is from a book, *Theocriti Aliorumque Poetarum Ilyllia,* to which Herbert may have had access, published in 1569:

5.

Comparing the visual aspects of this poem and the first print version of "Easter-wings," we see a clear visual connection between both "wings" poems. Brown and Ingoldsby state that "Herbert would almost certainly have been aware" (462) of this poem, as it had been printed and re-printed in several Renaissance anthologies. And Herbert was practiced in both Latin and Greek. Simmias also had written an altar-shaped poem—longer, but visually similar to Herbert's "Altar" along with a number of other pattern poems.

Beyond the visual similarity to Herbert's poem (the poem contracts with each line until it expands out again in equal measure), Simmias's

"Wings" is a song of praise to a winged God of love, albeit a pagan one. This prose translation of the poem features Cupid as Creator:

> Behold the ruler of the deep-bosomed Earth, the turner upside-down of the Son of Acmon, and have no fear that so little a person should have so plentiful a crop of beard to his chin. For I was born when Necessity bare rule, and all creatures, moved they in Air or in Chaos, were kept though her dismal governance far apart. Swift-flying son of Cypris and war-lord Ares – I am not that at all; for by no force came I into rule, but by gentle-willed persuasion, and yet all alike, Earth, deep Sea, and brazen Heaven, bowed to my behest, and I took to myself their old sceptre and made me a judge among gods (Edmunds 493).

In a private correspondence, classicist and poet A.E. Stallings pointed out to me that Simmias's "Wings" is "a meditation on the two biographies of Eros—one has him (Cupid) as this child of Aphrodite, a kind of mischievous, winged boy. But in the *Theogony* he is initially among the most ancient of the gods, descended directly from the initial state of Chaos, and nothing can come into being without him" (Stallings). I would argue that Herbert's poem also imagines a deity of love (though not Eros) in two complementary biographies, if you will: one as incarnated God, and another as crucified God. In these wing poems by Simmias and Herbert, we see two types of love, Eros and Agape, respectively, as Creators of the world. However, though Cupid may shoot the arrows of love into us, Christ receives the wounds from us, on our behalf, for love. The Simmias poem ultimately argues that Eros was there at the creation of the world. In a similar way, John 1 argues that all things were made by Him, the Word, Jesus. Herbert's first line includes the word "createdst," while Simmias's poem ends by noting a god's creative power. These things could be coincidence, but it seems likely that part of Herbert's impetus in writing "Easter-wings" was as a Christian response to Simmias's pagan poem.

Brown and Ingoldsby point out a remarkable difference in that Simmias's poem has six-line wings and Herbert's wings are made of five lines, the longest of which has ten syllables. Formally, they show, this architecture aligns with (rather than a pagan Cherub) the winged cherubim described in I Kings 6:23–27: five cubits in length of wing, ten cubits in all (466). Inside Solomon's sanctuary two winged gold-plated olive-wood cherubim stood, and this image parallels Herbert's poetic architecture made up of two sets of wings rather than Simmias's one set. For Herbert, there may be two reasons to give support to this shape. First, these two cherubim surrounded the presence of God held by the ark. Second, as we know from the gospel accounts of the empty tomb, two angels were present at the empty sepulcher of the risen Christ. In the gospels, we have an interesting paradox: the absence of the body at the tomb indicates the presence of God's power through resurrection. Thus, Herbert's poem's strict numerical pattern and shape shows both Hebrew and Greek influence in regards to angelic beings. Random Cloud (a playful pseudonym for the scholar Randall McLeod), in a 111-page article on "Easter-wings," argues that there are two "Easter-wings" poems rather than one poem made of two stanzas. After all, the title appears on both pages of early printed books and the first manuscripts. The other poems in the manuscripts do not have the title printed where the poems continue on the following pages. Two titles of "Easter-wings" (one on each page) supports Cloud's notion that there are two independent poems being represented by these shapes (84, 85).

Herbert's poetic play extends beyond the formal or shapely and into the semantic. An odd phrase in this last stanza might need illuminating: "if I imp my wing on thine." The word *imp* comes from the idiom of falconry. To imp means to graft feathers (from another bird) onto the wing of a trained falcon or hawk in order to repair damage and/or increase flying capacity. In the context of this poem, how can we make sense of this metaphor? Is God like a raptor? Can God be damaged or wounded? In the example of Christ, the answer is a resounding yes. We know the metaphor of an eagle is used to show God's mastery of the heavens several times in the scriptures. Deuteronomy 32:11–12 declares of God's people: "As an eagle stirs up its nest, / Hovers over its young, / Spreading out its wings, taking them up, / Carrying them on its wings, So the Lord alone led him / and there was no foreign god with him." And Exodus 19:4 states, "You have seen what I did to the Egyptians, and how I bore you on eagle's wings and brought you to myself." And just as the Hebrew scriptures provide for Herbert's raptor imagery, the New Testament gospels and letters offer precedents for the notion of grafting. Paul declares in Romans 11:17 that Gentiles can be grafted into the main branch to partake of the covenant that had been promised to the Jews. This picture of grafting is a metaphor for salvation and new life that demands a connection to a source of life.

It is not in its overt moments of scriptural allusion alone that Herbert's poem suggests a connection between Christ and wings. The very shape of the poem in its original layout encodes a profound theological argument into the shape of wings. The hourglass shape of the Simmias poem is most commonly how we see Herbert's poem re-presented (just perform a Google search for an "Easter-wings" image, and you can see that the poem is nearly always centered). But if one revisits the manuscript versions, one can see that this layout may not have been Herbert's original intent. While the shape of an hourglass does prove meaningful by imagistically presenting issues of time and death, and while it does seem that Herbert knew Simmias's shape poem as well as the shape of it, the first printed shape of "Easter-wings" is perhaps merely the wish of the printer to have it so. The manuscript versions suggest a formal organization that is justified to the right margin of the page, especially the Williams manuscript version of "Easter-wings." Why not perfectly right-justified? One only need imagine oneself as an amanuensis trying to re-copy Herbert's poem. In English writing, we compose left to write. If we are trying to end on the right side of the page, where do we begin on the left? It may not be possible, without some distortion of the size of the hand, to make it line up exactly on the right. These vicissitudes of handwriting might explain the slight curvature of the shape to be only a minor accident. The right side of the second stanza of the Williams manuscript is hardly curved at all and nearly perfectly right-justified.

If Herbert's poem were printed as we have in the manuscripts, right-justified, it would still display two wings, but the flatness of the right margin would make the shape less convincing as a natural form. However, consider the empty space created on the left side of the page by the absence of ink. If printed this way, this clean whiteness of the paper (the absence of the text) might be seen as a wing rounded and extending, tapering from left to right.

Now let us imagine what this inverted view might mean symbolically. Christians serve an invisible God yet have faith in His presence, though it cannot be seen. Hebrews 11 proclaims that "faith is the substance of things hoped for, the evidence of things not seen." We have on this page, in the shape left by the absence of the words, a kind of evidence of things not seen. I can imagine the humble poet thinking that if he imps his wing (representative of his own limited lark-song) upon God's invisibility, then God is glorified. God's absence is only a human inability to see Him. In his weakness, the poet is made strong. After Christ has departed the earth, Paul instructs his readers to imagine themselves as the body of Christ (I Corinthians 12). Herbert's poem partakes in a higher and more powerful artistic calling by unifying with God in this sharing of feathers/wings and word/Word. Also, we have as a proof of the risen Christ an absence: the empty tomb. One can look at the manuscript versions of the poem and see the white space acting as that stone rolled away here for us to witness a holy emptiness. Most poore. Most thinne. Yet, *With Thee*. "With Thee" is the only line repeated exactly in both stanzas, emphasizing its urgency. It is visually the hinge on which the poem turns, twice. Our mortal life in a fallen world can be rectified and restored only "With Thee." Finally, the falcon is never mentioned directly. It is technically absent, but present through the words "imp my wing on Thine." This metaphorical raptor is present only through the verb "imp." This varying absence and presence of the wing, or feathers, is essential to our understanding of the poem's shape.

Considering the various shapes in which "Easter-wings" has been presented, especially early on, it seems no less than astonishing that one of the most famous shape-poems in English is most often read in a form that Herbert may not have intended. One thing is clear: the centered, first print version looks much more like the Simmias "Wings" poem and much less like the two handwritten versions of "Easter-wings."

The Little Gidding workers produced versions of scripture called Biblical Harmonies, which combined numerous printed versions of Biblical writings into altered works of text/art. Various scriptures and images from multiple texts were cut up, glued, and laid side-by-side on pages to produce works that displayed comparisons/compositions of verses and images alongside and blended with one another. One of these versions was given to Herbert around 1631, and Herbert had a "high prizeing of it & thank full acknowledgmt for it" (Smyth 463). If the Little Gidding printers were willing to deconstruct and reconstruct a Bible to create new versions, it is possible they felt an artistic permission to reconstruct the shape of Herbert's "Easter-wings" to finally center it rather than leave it right-justified.

The right-justified version of the printed "Easter-wings" poems (closest to how the manuscripts look—with the empty spaces of two white wings) would appear something like this:

Easter-wings

Lord, who createdst man in wealth and store,
Though foolishly he lost the same,
Decaying more and more,
Till he became
Most poore:
With thee
O let me rise
As larks, harmoniously,
And sing this day thy victories:
Then shall the fall further the flight in me.

Easter-wings

My tender age in sorrow did beginne
And still with sicknesses and shame
Thou didst so punish sinne,
That I became
Most thinne.
With thee
Let me combine,
And feel thy victorie:
For, if I imp my wing on thine,
Affliction shall advance the flight in me.

To be more faithful to the shapes of the two early manuscripts, I believe future reproductions of "Easter-wings" should look something close to this layout. You can see that with this presentation, the two big emptinesses cutting from the left side into the stanzas are now a bit more startling and meaningful. As I argued earlier, the paradox of absence as presence is now much more emphasized, and the invisible is made visible via the greater area of negative space. Notice how the words make the white shape visible; in Christianity, the Word makes the invisible God visible.

Joan Bennett has written about the effect of the rise and fall and subsequent rise/resurrection in the larks' song and flight, imitated imagistically by Herbert's form, though she does perceive him as a minor poet: "despite his aristocratic birth and breeding and his considerable learning, leaves the impression of an unsophisticated mind" (63). She sees his play with shape and anagrams as childish in comparison to Donne's formal achievements, not seeming to fathom how Herbert correlates his formal decisions with his content in such complex ways. In another poem of Herbert's, "Church-musick," a praise song is illustrated once again by using bird imagery as a vehicle through which one can be lost metaphysically in the greater glory of heavenly power: "Now I in you without a bodie move, / Rising and falling with your wings" (5–6). But in "Easter-wings," note that Herbert never mentions the falcon directly. He is technically absent, only present through the words "imp my wing on Thine." This metaphorical raptor is present only through the verb "imp." This varying absence and presence of the feather, or wing, is essential to our understanding of the poem's shape.

There is even more to the bird imagery. If Herbert (or any poet-singer) is one of the "larks" (line 8), and feathers from the wings of those larks (first stanza) are grafted onto a damaged wing of the raptor (second stanza), then it seems that a diminutive lark can partake of a greater glory—not only to sing a song of praise, but to experience God's greater power of mastering the air. Rather than focus on the natural ability of the raptor to overtake the lark and consume it, the poet allows the lark to partake, via the grafting, of the raptor's greater power of flight. "If I imp my wing on thine" is the sacrifice required. For the Christian, to lose one's life is to find it. In "Easter-wings," Herbert has made clear to us in several ways that "To live is Christ, and to die is gain" (Philippians 1:21). To say finally "Affliction shall advance the flight in me" points to the supreme suffering on the cross. If we are spiritually grafted into that place of his wound, into a proven immortal body, then we can be a part of the body of that powerful falcon (the one who has the power over the life of the other). Even as "sons" born into this world of sorrow, we are in need of being grafted into something greater to achieve our greatest potential. Note also that the falcon is wounded if it requires "imping." The metaphor of the falcon in "Easter-wings" is even more meaningful when we recognize how a centurion's spear left a gaping wound in Christ's side, confirming his death. The disciple Thomas thrusting his hand into Jesus' side post-resurrection can be seen as a metaphorical example of grafting. His own doubt (his absence of faith) is allowed and encouraged to touch that famous wound.

Christians believe we each have our own sufferings, failures, and limitations where we can connect to the experience of God's suffering through the person of Jesus. The French theologian Simone Weil writes eloquently about this: "Men struck down by affliction are at the foot of the Cross, almost at the greatest possible distance from God" (83). To Weil, this affliction is of the greatest value. "In this marvelous dimension, the soul, without leaving the place and the instant where the body to which it is united is situated, can cross the totality of space and time and come into the very presence of God. It is at the intersection of creation and its Creator. This point of intersection is the point of intersection of the arms of the Cross" (94). George Herbert's own five-part poem (or five poems) entitled "Affliction (I-V)," shows a mind and heart constantly torn due to the multiplicity of failures inherent in the mortal and inconstant speaker. Just as the shape of "Easter-wings" both diminishes and expands again, so do Herbert's hopes violently swing between joy and despair in these beautiful lines. One example of the extreme conflict of heart and mind Herbert feels is portrayed in the final rhyming couplet of "Affliction I": "Ah my deare God! though I am clean forgot, / Let me not love thee, if I love thee not" (65–66). As he admits his failures and seeks God's restoration, Herbert seems to realize that the limitations of human love can be answered only by an immortal love that once partook of this grief.

The totality of "Easter-wings" likewise suggests to us that instead of being merely singers, or even devoured prey, it is possible to share in God's glory. One can be grafted into a greater eternal life, already risen. "With thee," as George Herbert puts it, is perhaps the only hope for a meaningful answer to the curse of mortality and a way for the fallen and afflicted to abide in the Almighty God.

Bibliography

Bennet, Joan. Five Metaphysical Poets. Cambridge: Cambridge University Press, 1966.

Brown, C.C. and Ingoldsby, W.P. "George Herbert's 'Easter Wings'." *Essential Articles for the Study of George Herbert's Poetry*. Hamden, CT: Archon Books, 1979, pp. 461–472.

Charles, Amy. *The Williams Manuscript of George Herbert's Poems: A Facsimile Reproduction*. New York: Delmar Press, 1977.

Cloud, Random. "FIAT *f*LUX," in Randall M Leod, ed., *Crisis in Editing: Texts of the English Renaissance*. New York: AMS Press, 1994.

Di Cesare, Mario. *George Herbert, The Temple: A Diplomatic Edition of the Bodleian Manuscript* (Tanner 307). Binghamton, NY: Medieval & Renaissance Texts & Studies, 1995.

Edmonds, J.M. *The Greek Bucolic Poets*. New York: The MacMillan Company, 1912.

Halli, Robert W. Jr. "The Double Hieroglyph in George Herbert's 'Easter-Wings.'" *Philological Quarterly* 63 (1984): 265–272.

Lull, Janice. *The Poem in Time: Reading George Herbert's Revisions of The Church*. Newark: University of Delaware Press, 1990.

Smyth, Adam. "'Shreds of holinesse': George Herbert, Little Gidding, and Cutting Up Texts in Early Modern England." *English Literary Renaissance* 42 (2012): 452–481.

Stallings, A.E. Private email correspondence. August 5, 2017.

Vendler, Helen. *The Poetry of George Herbert.* Cambridge, MA: Harvard University Press, 1975.

Weil, Simone. *Waiting on God.* London: Collins, 1959.

Image descriptions:

1. "Easter-wings" from *The Works of George Herbert,* Oxford University, Oxford. 1914.
2. "Easter-wings" from *The temple. Sacred poems and private ejaculations.* By Mr. George Herbert, late oratour of the Universitie of Cambridge, pp. 34v—35r 1633. (Courtesy Wrenn Library Collection of the Harry Ransom Center, Austin, TX).
3. "Easter-wings" by George Herbert from MS. Jones B-62 pp. 27v—28r. (Courtesy Dr. Williams Library, London).
4. "Easter-wings" by George Herbert from MS. Tanner 307 pp. 27v—28r (Courtesy The Bodleian Library, London).
5. "Wings" by Simmias of Rhodes from *Theocriti aliorumque poetarum Idyllia : Eiusdem Epigrammata. Simmiae Rhodii Ouum,* Alae. 1569 (Courtesy Duke University Library, Duke, NC).

Patience in Poetry

Just outside Lubbock, Texas, there is an architectural wonder known as the Robert Bruno House. It is a house built of thick steel plates on the crumbling cliff's edge looming over Ransom Canyon. Rising from its four curving support legs with rooms jutting like great bug's eyes here and there, the rusted steel shell of the house seems some kind of space creature or galactic outpost, part animal and part machine. It hovers there on the edge of the cliff, making a mockery of the cookie cutter brick homes in the canyon below. Robert Bruno began construction of the house in 1974 and had just moved into the house in 2008, when later that same year the cancer he had been battling finally led to complications that killed him.

Bruno was denied tenure in the early 1980s by Texas Tech University, my own employer. He continued to teach as an adjunct professor and build the house, also working on other projects and apparently designing solar/irrigation systems for farming to create an income.

On three or four visits to the house over the years, I stopped by and was lucky to find him at work and willing to talk about the house and art and West Texas. On one of the early visits, I had come upon him hand-sanding a piece of beautiful wood he had acquired from South America; it was only one of many steps in a spiral staircase at the center of the house. He had been at work on the house for thirty years and hadn't moved in yet, and here he was sanding a piece of wood that would eventually take its place virtually unnoticed in this monstrous achievement. While he gently moved this piece of sandpaper back and forth over the wood, he told me he would soon have electricity and water running to the house. I asked him if he ever had any help, as it seemed to me he might accelerate getting moved in. He said that, yes, he had hired some help over the years, but others rarely seemed to do things the way he wanted them done, and he enjoyed doing it himself. And he didn't think about it as only a house, because he could really live anywhere else. This was something aesthetic. He had time for that.

***

The appreciation of the great poets, T.S. Eliot says, "is a lifetime's task, because at every stage of maturing…you are able to understand them better." For Eliot these poets were Shakespeare, Dante, Homer, and Virgil. Outside the task of taking on such expansive poets, any reader must take time to read a good poem. Unless lodged within the confines of a classroom, many will not set aside fifteen minutes for a poem. Yet Eliot calls for "a lifetime's task." Many things distract us from poetry, yet never has there been more access to it. The one thing that remains the same is the length of time it takes to read a poem. However, it may be that contemporary readers need to take more time due to the measurable diminishment of reading skills that has beset us in the past few decades. I use the phrase, "take time." I might have written, "make time." What do we do with time? We "carve out time" or "waste time" or "spend time." I shudder when people use the expression, "kill time." Time kills us, but we cannot retaliate. I like the phrase "find time," as it hints at discovery. Yet to "make time" (usually a phrase that we consider conciliatory) would be a more creative achievement.

There are poems that we read in minutes. They are like most Hollywood entertainment. You witness them, perhaps some small epiphany, and then you are done. You leave the page or the movie theater and move on to the next thing. But with a good film, you leave the theater reflecting on what just happened to you, how the characters, the plot, the cinematography or even the costumes not only mirror but impinge upon your life, and this meditation continues well past the drive home and on through the next morning's coffee. In a letter to Robert Lowell, Elizabeth Bishop wrote that she knew she had read a good poem when for the next twenty-four hours the world looked like that poem. Who hasn't had their world affected in this way by some form of art?

Longsuffering is a word no longer in common use, and I believe this lack diminishes our human condition. We only think to use the word *patience*, though there is a discernible difference. Colossians 1:10–11 reads:

> that you may walk worthy of the Lord, fully pleasing *Him*, being fruitful in every good work and increasing in the knowledge of God; strengthened with all might, according to His glorious power, for all patience and longsuffering with joy.

Patience and *longsuffering*, since they are mentioned in this passage of Colossians at once, cannot mean the same thing. The two words in the Greek here are *hupomone* and *makrothumia*. *Hupomone* is literally "abiding under" and *makrothumia* something like "far or long wrath." Both terms spatially position the person in relation to adversity, difficulty, or whatever situation might be at hand, the first vertically and the second horizontally. Clearly, *makrothumia* (longsuffering) has embedded within itself the source of affliction, a more difficult sense of waiting.

Which brings us to Simone Weil who said a number of poignant things about the extreme suffering which she calls *malheur*, or affliction. One of these: "And if we conceive the fullness of joy, suffering is still to joy what hunger is to food." She has written so powerfully about this matter, I can add little to it, so I recommend you to her marvelous essay, "The Love of God and Affliction."

What are the differences between patience and longsuffering and affliction, all different gradations of difficulty in waiting, the last being nearly impossible to bear? Weil says, "Affliction is ridiculous." She asserts that it is, however, one of the only ways we can truly come to share in the glory of the cross. If affliction reaches beyond longsuffering and brings us into communion with the greatest of passions, then we can see how useless is the desire of our age: instant gratification. In fact, if we could notice the degree in which we are showered with instant gratification, we might come to see the perversity of our present culture. Rather than this negative response to difficulty and the failure to understand suffering's very nature, we might participate in the wonder of waiting on God.

I don't really like to talk about my chronic back pain. It sometimes moves me to the realm of affliction. I know that my affliction has purpose, but that faith provides little comfort. While I don't and probably can't know now exactly what that purpose is, I do see myself having a greater heart for those who suffer chronic physical pain. And that is still a moral choice one has to make, especially when one considers the thief hanging beside Jesus who could only despise his two fellow sufferers, one of them who had done no wrong. As a believer I have the hope that, ultimately, I will see the pain's purpose, both practically and spiritually.

But Weil says that one shouldn't try to find value in affliction because it has purpose; only because it is. Affliction *is*, connecting me to the One who hung on a cross in unfathomable pain on my behalf, and then suffered all that other emotional and spiritual pain that far surpasses mine so He could know who I am. Or to put it another way, so that *I* could know that *He* knows who I am. I consider this a state of being or abiding, and not a lesson learned. But I don't want to address affliction or even patience here.

I want to examine that mysterious middle ground of longsuffering, by which I mean: the calm, uncomplaining endurance of a difficulty. Weil speaks much more directly of longsuffering in her essay "Reflection on the Right Use of School Studies with a View to the Love of God." The title reveals much, as does the first sentence: "The key to a Christian conception of studies is the realization that prayer consists of attention." Her essay details how education prepares us by training this power of attention toward scholastic knowledge so that we might gain a sort of practice toward prayer. Even if we fail in some particular area, she says, if we have given our full attention to a matter, we have succeeded. Ultimately, this kind of attention embraces humility and patience, and it stifles pride. She claims "We do not obtain the most precious gifts by going in search of them but by waiting for them."

***

But what does this have to do with poetry? Well, poetry is a pain, and it takes time. This is the poet's "necessary laziness" of which T.S. Eliot spoke. Lorca, in his famous essay on "Duende" says: "In the room was Ignacio Espeleta, handsome as a Roman tortoise, who was once asked: 'Why don't you work?' and who replied with a smile worthy of Argantonius: 'How should I work, if I'm from Cádiz?'" Elizabeth Bishop's writing of "The Moose" illustrates a kind of patience most of us couldn't muster in these "publish or perish" times. She worked on and off, revising that poem for nearly thirty years since its first inception some time around 1946. Many poets these days are under such pressure to publish that they don't hold back a good version of a poem for more than a month to finish it. But when we read the final version of "The Moose," we are happy that Bishop had the extraordinary patience for such a work to materialize.

Written in occasionally-rhymed sexains, the event of the poem is a study in patience, a bus trip from Nova Scotia to Boston. And during the trip a moose steps into the road, delaying the journey. But no one seems upset about the postponement. This barricade of a moose creates a marvelous moment where the natural world has overpowered the world of humans and has suspended time. Even when the bus pulls away, there is a "craning backward," a longing for the moment to stay. And the moment does linger even longer due to a "dim / smell of moose" carried with the travelers. Here we end with the sense of smell which many have suggested most strongly evokes the faculty of memory.

Knowing of decades-long compositions, literary precedents such as Bishop's "The Moose" and others like it, I am encouraged to wait patiently for some of my poems to mature. If a poet can embrace a little humility, he realizes that just about any poem he has written will get better with time and the revision and perspective that time allows. Sometimes this outlook is achieved through time via rejection of the work by publishers. If a poem has been rejected enough, one begins to gain a little perspective on it, a little objectivity through time passing, and perhaps one sees a poor repetition in the work, a forced rhyme, or a clichéd perception, or perhaps one even finds a direction the poem really wanted to go, that surprise for the writer that now can become the surprise for the reader, as Robert Frost puts it.

But it is hard to get poems written. If one can understand poetry as art, as any other art, one understands the work it will take to produce something of value. Compare it to music or painting. Few untrained persons will sit down to a piano or guitar and bang out a tune and call it great art. Few can succeed in the visual arts if they don't prepare themselves in the drawing of a straight line or come via experience to understand how paint reacts, runs, blends, and dries on a variety of media at the hand of a variety of trowels or brushes, or even understanding a lovely color palette. Yet countless scribblers every day will sit down with no formal training whatsoever, with never having even read a poem closely, and then rise with notebook in hand claiming to have written a poem because they had a feeling they wanted to express.

The difference between various art practices is probably obvious. We use language all the time, and by our twenties we have two decades of experience, perhaps have a penchant or a knack for arranging the words just so, whereas the wannabe musician has probably experienced little use of the instrument there. And poets have feelings! But poetry is neither simply

196

feeling nor mere conversational language. The presence of artifice and deeply complex aesthetic choices distinguishes poetry from feeling and thought and common speech.

Recently, a senior in one of our more intense discussions asked the class earnestly, "Who's to say if Dante or Shakespeare is better than anybody writing today?" With no verbal response from the other students, I replied as kindly as possible, "I'm to say. Any poet who has developed a sense of taste is to say." And then I began, as I had done before, listing the parts that make up the whole of poetry: diction, syntax, grammar, sound, rhythm, imagery, rhetoric, abstraction, verbs, nouns, prepositions, etc., and these parts organized in such a fashion that the machine at hand produces some moving effect. Like a vehicle. You have some poems that are space shuttles and some that are go-karts. And some look like vehicles, but they don't really run at all.

You only need to read Eliot's "Tradition and the Individual Talent" for a very straightforward idea of how this works:

> It cannot be inherited, and if you want it you must obtain it by great labour. It involves, in the first place, the historical sense, which we may call nearly indispensable to anyone who would continue to be a poet beyond his twenty-fifth year; and the historical sense involves a perception, not only of the pastness of the past, but of its presence; the historical sense compels a man to write not merely with his own generation in his bones, but with a feeling that the whole of the literature of Europe from Homer and within it the whole of the literature of his own country has a simultaneous existence and composes a simultaneous order.

In this brief and famous essay, Eliot also understands that poets need to harbor a certain "necessary laziness" in order not to be merely pedantic and admits "that much learning deadens or perverts poetic sensibility." And we know that the business of poetry and "po-biz" are just two more busynesses that can distract us from the patient beauty we might achieve in writing a poem. What I mean to say here is that work and longsuffering go hand in hand, whereas busyness tends to strive against both.

Yeats, in "Adam's Curse," captures the sense of longsuffering in poetry:

... "To be born woman is to know —
Although they do not talk of it at school —
That we must labour to be beautiful."
I said, "It's certain there is no fine thing
Since Adam's fall but needs much labouring.
There have been lovers who thought love should be
So much compounded of high courtesy
That they would sigh and quote with learned looks
precedents out of beautiful old books;
Yet now it seems an idle trade enough.

"An idle trade"! Love as business, or what we call prostitution, a mere sexual exchange rather than that courtly recognition that love is difficult and beautiful.

Who wants to labor? In English, both senses of the word, for male and female, are the curses (along with death) rewarded for our first disobedience: pain in childbirth and the toil of the land. Labor. The difficulty of being fruitful. It's interesting, isn't it? The curse for partaking of forbidden fruit is the difficulty of being fruitful. Most pregnant women in Lubbock these days opt for the epidural. My wife, my hero, opted for the pain. It is a heroic act, going through labor. I can't say I would do it, and I don't disparage women who choose to numb the pain. But, as my wife says, "If you go through it, you can find out who you are."

Or who wants what Eliot prescribes: "the historical sense" of poetry? Wouldn't that take decades, and how can I be a poet now when I only know a little poetry? Many young students want to be poets only because they feel it. Which is enough for a start, I admit, as it was me. Yet no student approaches engineering that way; they have to understand math and physics, chemistry and dynamics. Ultimately, poetry requires understanding the fundamentals of language and enjoyment of the work, and a poet must embrace what we call "longsuffering" as if it's a virtue. As if it's a gift, or even a fruit of the Spirit.

***

I had gone to see Robert Bruno in the spring of his final year when I was working on a poem about Ransom Canyon. The poem is a poem in sections, and I knew that I wanted at least one of the sections to be about Bruno and his house. I deeply felt he and his work would be a part of the poem, but I didn't know how. So I wanted to talk to him. I approached the house, but there was a sign on the door which stated this was now a residence and for visitors to please go away. It startled me. I suddenly felt like a trespasser, and I backed away into the front yard bordering the street where my car waited. But I didn't want to go, and I'm glad I had the patience to wander about the yard and make some drawings and sit down next to my car to write some notes for my poem. His truck was there, but I wasn't sure if he was home.

I was getting ready to leave when Bruno came out and motioned for me to come to him. He invited me in, remembering me, that I was a poet. He showed me the recent updates and said something about having ten or twenty more years to go. I knew his cancer had been in remission, but somehow I imagined he knew he would never complete the house. He seemed content to do the work at hand.

The house is so utterly sculptural, I thought I'd engage him in conversation about his influences, whether it were Brancusi, or Picasso, or Braque or one of the Bauhaus artists. He looked at me strangely, silently, thinking for a long while. He said, "More music, really, than sculpture." He named a few classical composers and said he liked to model on the patterns in the music. That seemed to me at once wildly imaginative and reasonable.

He had recently installed some of the stained glass which fits into the internal structure of the house. He had designed the glass himself. He showed me the revised upper floor of the house, how he had moved a support beam and raised the entire upper floor about a foot in order to open up the room while getting a better view of both lakes that make up the basin of the canyon, Buffalo Springs Lake being just a bit higher than Lake Ransom Canyon. He told me that one alteration had set him back an entire year.

I tell this story of Robert Bruno to myself in order to try and get my head around a more patient way of making my own art and living my life.

I don't know the details of his daily routines or conflicts, but I do know he patiently worked at this house for over thirty years, some of it requiring patience and certainly longsuffering.

If I spent thirty years on a poem knowing I might not complete it, what might I achieve? W.H. Auden, anti-romantic that he is, points out that there will be no perfection of the life or the art. And Paul Valéry famously said that a poem is never finished, only abandoned. On the other hand, Christian Wiman has suggested that a poet might set out to build some ideal design and end up enamored of the scaffolding. I think it was the '90s when academia was favoring process over product. We still do, I'm sure, but sometimes not finishing a project often leaves you with ingredients rather than food.

Of course, I enjoy writing shorter lyric poems, and I have no designs on writing an epic. I did, oddly, get seventy thousand words into a novel this summer, but who knows what will come of that diversion to prose? Nevertheless, there is the body of my work—the French word, *oeuvre*. The work. The labor. The poems as a whole. Perhaps each stair step, each plate of steel, each stained-glass pane, each pain, might add up to a work that not only housed a life, but made the world beautiful and encouraged other lives toward that same endeavor.

Attributions

Auden, W. H. "As I Walked Out One Evening," © 1940 and © renewed 1968 from *COLLECTED POEMS* by W. H. Auden, edited by Edward Mendelson. Used by permission of Random House, an imprint and division of Penguin Random House LLC. All rights reserved. Also, reprinted by permission of Curtis Brown, Ltd.

Bishop, Elizabeth. "The Moose" from *POEMS*. © by the Alice H. Methfessel Trust. Publisher's Note and compilation © 2011. Reprinted by permission of Farrar, Straus, & Giroux. Also, "The Moose" published by Vintage. Reproduced by permission of The Random House Group Ltd. ©2012.

Brock, Geoffrey. "Exercitia Spiritualia" from *WEIGHING LIGHT*. p.14. © 2005. Reprinted with permission of the author.
Chang, Victoria. "I Once Was a Child" from *THE BOSS*. p. 1. © 2013. Reprinted with permission of the author.

Larkin, Philip. "Church Going" from *THE COMPLETE POEMS OF PHILIP LARKIN*, edited by Archie Burnett. © 2012 by The Estate of Philip Larkin. Reprinted by permission of Farrar, Straus, & Giroux and Faber and Faber Limited.

Martin, Charles. "After 9/11" from *SIGNS & WONDERS*. pp. 63–68. © 2011 Johns Hopkins University Press. Reprinted with permission of Johns Hopkins University Press.

Spaar, Lisa Russ. "Watch" from *VANITAS, ROUGH*. p. 56. © 2012. Reprinted with permission from the author.